FAITH CONQUERS ASHES

This novel is a work of fiction. However, several names, descriptions, entities, and incidents included in the story are based on the lives of real people.

The opinions expressed by the author are not necessarily those of Tate Publishing, LLC.

Published by Tate Publishing & Enterprises, LLC
127 E. Trade Center Terrace | Mustang, Oklahoma 73064 USA
1.888.361.9473 | www.tatepublishing.com

Tate Publishing is committed to excellence in the publishing industry. The company reflects the philosophy established by the founders, based on Psalm 68:11,
"The Lord gave the word and great was the company of those who published it."

Cover design by Stephen C. Violette
Interior design by Mary Jean Archival

Published in the United States of America

ISBN: 978-1-62902-485-1
True Crime / Murder
13.12.10

DEDICATION

This book is dedicated to God, our Heavenly Father and Supreme Creator, in memory of my sister, Jennifer. I'm convinced it's because of His supreme love and guidance that Jennifer's body was returned to us and so many incredible answers to our prayers were delivered. Those answered prayers could never have been earned, as no human could ever be worthy or good enough to earn them. And I'm reminded daily that only through the grace of God and the love of our savior, Jesus Christ, were we allowed the blessing of being able to bury her and move forward in our lives. I hope and pray the sharing of these amazing answers will please Him.

The one major regret I have, however, is that I never got to meet Jennifer. She was just a baby when I moved away. But I do remember seeing several pictures of her at different ages. Of course I flew back to Oklahoma to attend Jenny's funeral to be there for my best friend as she mourned the loss of her baby sister. I was invited to sit with the family in the front row during the service. Some of the family wore a silver memory bracelet in Jennifer's honor embossed with "Jennifer ~ In Loving Memory." One song I remember especially. It was written by one of her dad's friends called, "PromiseLand" also known as "Jenny's Song." The lyrics and melody seemed to lift everyone's spirits as they imagined Jennifer existing in the beautifully described heavenly place.

As you read this book, imagine what it must have been like happening to any family, let alone a close friend. Let her family and their faith lift you to a closer path with the Lord. Receive the gift of seeing answers to prayer. Above all, know the Lord reigns!

Sheila A. Smith

DEDICATION

This book is dedicated to God, our Heavenly Father and Supreme Creator, in memory of my sister, Jennifer. I'm convinced it's because of His supreme love and guidance that Jennifer's body was returned to us and so many incredible answers to our prayers were delivered. Those answered prayers could never have been earned, as no human could ever be worthy or good enough to earn them. And I'm reminded daily that only through the grace of God and the love of our savior, Jesus Christ, were we allowed the blessing of being able to bury her and move forward in our lives. I hope and pray the sharing of these amazing answers will please Him.

SPECIAL FORWARD BY SHEILA A. SMITH

It is an honor to write this special forward to this book but I'm deeply saddened by the reason for it. It's hard to believe I've known the author, Mary, and her family, for almost 30 years! We've been through a lot together and I thank God for our fabulous gift of friendship.

Our friendship began many years ago, carrying us on a magnificent journey through life and the raising of our children. We've shared many similar experiences, including the loss of a sister. And we believe so many similarities between our two lives mean we were meant to cross paths. In fact, we believe God intended for us to meet all those years ago at the office building where we worked. Since then, we've laughed together plenty of times about the long list of similarities we share. And even though we've been separated by moves throughout the years due to job changes, we've kept in touch both by letter and phone. Our friendship has not only survived but has thrived! We believe we are kindred spirits in the Lord. We've talked for hours on the phone, regularly, sharing our hopes and dreams, along with the normal struggles of daily living.

The one major regret I have, however, is that I never got to meet Jennifer. She was just a baby when I moved away. But I do remember seeing several pictures of her at different ages. Of course I flew back to Oklahoma to attend Jenny's funeral to be there for my best friend as she mourned the loss of her baby sister. I was invited to sit with the family in the front row during the service. Some of the family wore a silver memory bracelet in Jennifer's honor embossed with "Jennifer ~ In Loving Memory." One song I remember especially. It was written by one of her dad's friends called, "PromiseLand" also known as "Jenny's Song." The lyrics and melody seemed to lift everyone's spirits as they imagined Jennifer existing in the beautifully described heavenly place.

As you read this book, imagine what it must have been like happening to any family, let alone a close friend. Let her family and their faith lift you to a closer path with the Lord. Receive the gift of seeing answers to prayer. Above all, know the Lord reigns!

Sheila A. Smith

JENNIFER

The heavens opened up
and a star came falling down.
I followed with my eyes
and even found it, on the ground.
And when I knelt to touch it
and gaze upon it's glow,
it sparkled and a gentle heartbeat throbbed
there on the snow.

It lay there for a moment
expecting me to cry,
as if she knew I'd recognize her
falling through the sky.
I didn't cry and didn't grieve;
I knew she came for me,
to say "I never left you
but now my spirit's free."

Mary Perryman
November 18, 2008

CONTENTS

SHOCK AND HORROR

AUGUST 3, 2006

The afternoon drive was brutal, without mentioning the heat! The sweat, forming under my arms and at the back of my neck, threatened to soak my blouse. It was a typically hot August day in Oklahoma, and having a broken air conditioner in my car didn't make it a pleasant ride home. Plus, Mom kept flashing through my mind. "Just keep moving, Mary, keep the breeze flowing through the car," I told myself. It was only 4:35 p.m. and I was already gritting my teeth and humming an agitated tune. It had to be 150 degrees inside, and here I was, stuck in a hot car with no AC. I heard the usual horns honking and watched the other drivers rudely barge in and out, weaving between other cars while jockeying for position, causing near accidents on the highway. What a crazy, irritating drive home from work!

I just wanted to get home and get there early for a change. I thought of my mom, wondering what kind of day she'd had. Had she cried all day, refusing to leave her home? I knew she practically sat by the phone, waiting for Jennifer to call, waiting for a call that just never came. I made a mental note to call and check on her as soon as

I got home. I could imagine her anticipation every time her phone rang. I hated to disappoint her.

"Call her, Mary, but don't ask if she's heard anything about Jennifer today," I instructed myself. I knew Mom was one step away from a major breakdown since Jenny's disappearance eight long months ago. And I knew she must be tired of people asking, "Has anyone heard from Jennifer? Has she called anyone? Has anyone seen Jennifer?" The constant reminder of what my mother no longer had near her took its toll. Her crying spells, the constant sleeping, and the general disinterest in life made my heart bleed for her. I missed Jennifer too, but I could see Jenny's absence was *killing* our mother. *God, please just give us her body back!* I'd prayed daily. I knew something bad must have happened to her since we'd last seen her, Thanksgiving of 2005. No one heard from her, saw her, or knew any clue where she could be. Then there was the dream I had. It clearly convinced me she was dead. All I needed for proof was her body. If only we had it!

"Awesome! I'm early!" I congratulated myself as I turned the car into the driveway. "No speeding required." I laughed out loud. But today, there were no errands to run either. That in itself was very unusual. I couldn't remember when I'd recently been home in time for the five o'clock evening news. My furry "kids" greeted me at the door, rubbing their cotton-soft heads against my legs and begging to be petted. Two experienced nags, they're rotten and have trained me well, expecting me to know by the sound of their meows exactly what they want. They tag teamed me before I could even toss my lunch bag on the kitchen counter, and I remembered how Jenny and I *both* loved cats. An image of her holding her calico girl,

Sparkle, popped into my head. I glanced at the clock and noticed it was only 4:55 p.m. Woo-hoo! I'd made it home just in time.

I'm a news junkie but rarely get to see the whole broadcast of the five o'clock edition, so I was elated. I'd heard (earlier in the summer) of body parts being found in certain lake areas of Oklahoma and wondered if someone would ever find my sister. I prayed they would, but not in pieces! I couldn't think of anything more painful. Besides, I firmly believed God would lead someone to find her, and she would be returned to our family. I just couldn't allow myself to imagine the details of her return. As it turned out, I was right. She *would* be returned to us, and the Lord had a hand in the whole thing.

I half skipped over to my comfy old mauve rocking chair, feeling the cool air flow through the house, covering me, granting instant relief, and calming me all the way to my toes. I stood there, near the chair, lifting the remote control and aiming it toward the television. Strangely, I remember thinking, *Why am I in such a hurry to get the TV turned on? I haven't even put my purse down yet or taken off my shoes.* Yet I stood there, not bothering to sit down and get comfortable. Something inside led me to simply turn it on and stand, waiting. I did. *Click!* The television came into focus, and instantly, I saw a shape sitting on a desk or table. Whatever the shape sat on didn't matter. The object itself shocked, horrified, and paralyzed me!

It was a *head*, a human head with fake skin, hair, and eyes. But it wasn't just any head. The obvious reconstruction was someone I knew! I dropped my purse and felt my legs weaken and life drain out of my face and hands. I remember hearing someone on TV announce police were trying to obtain the identity of this person's remains.

Transfixed at the TV screen, I heard the scream inside my head, "No! God please don't let it be her!" I simply couldn't accept what I was seeing. The head sitting on the desk stared morbidly ahead, into nothingness. As the news crew zoomed out for a broader view of the room, I noticed the broadcast was being held from inside the Edmond police station.

Her rubber hair was short, just covering her head with a few strands covering her ears and reaching toward her neck. In sheer horror I stared, unable to take my eyes off the one I'd longed to see for eight long months. I felt odd; my skin wet with cold sweat and my body shaking uncontrollably. The almond-shaped eyes, the unmistakable nose and lips, the strong jaw line with the defiant chin, all belonged to *her*. The shock was overwhelming! I reached for the phone and called one of my other sisters, Jackie.

"Hello?" she answered, calmly.

"Jackie, where are you?" I asked frantically. I know she heard the urgency in my voice.

"Walking out the door to go to my cooking class," she replied. "What's wrong?"

"You need to go back in and turn your TV to channel nine," I told her in a pressing, yet pleading, tone.

I could hear her open the door and enter her house, still holding her cell phone. I heard her turn on her TV. Together we watched the remainder of the newscast until I asked the obvious question, "It's her, isn't it?"

"Uh-huh, it *looks* like her," she answered, slowly, reluctantly. I knew she didn't want it to be, but I knew we both believed it really was our youngest sister. "I'll call the police if you'll find their number for me," she said, mechanically. I could sense the tension building in her as she dealt with her shock.

I told her I'd try to find the number and laid down my cell phone. I noticed it flashed across the TV screen earlier, but I was too dazed to write it down. Desperation set in as I pawed through the business pages looking for the listing of the Edmond Police Department. The pages wouldn't turn, sticking together stubbornly and refusing to give up the information we needed.

"Come on! Come *on*! Where's the number?" I asked myself out loud, impatiently. The shaking was all encompassing, and I prayed, "God, please help me! I *know* this is Jennifer! Please help me find the page the number is on!" The pages finally released, giving the information we needed to get our lost sister back.

I reeled with the knowledge God had placed me in front of my TV at the precise moment I needed to be there. I'd always heard God's timing is perfect. Well, today he'd proven it to me for sure! No one else in our family might have seen this news. I gave Jackie the phone number along with one request.

"Jackie, just don't tell Mom yet, okay? Don't say anything to her until we have proof it's her," I begged before hanging up the phone. I felt weak. I couldn't bear the thought of our mother knowing what we'd found out, which suddenly in my mind became fact. I felt confident Mom hadn't seen the broadcast since she typically watched movies or one of her favorite sitcoms when she watched television. In my mind, our search for Jennifer was over.

I walked outside, pacing, and suddenly stopped, stunned with the realization both requests I'd given to God so far were answered! I remembered God answered my first prayer months ago when I'd prayed to be shown if Jennifer was alive or dead. He *had* shown me. Now he'd answered my second prayer through the media, to have her body back for burial. Prayer number two was answered! My heart felt like it would explode! I felt my body shake softly now, and the tears drip on to my shirt and arms. I couldn't erase the image I'd just seen on TV. A silent scream exploded inside my head, "No! You can't be dead! Don't go! Jennifer!"

REALITY SETS IN

The next few days sped by. Jennifer's dad Tommy (my stepfather, years earlier) flew back to Oklahoma from California, where he'd been living for several years following his divorce from our mother. Despite their failed marriage, Tommy and Mom had maintained a friendly relationship, parenting Jenny separately while she was growing up. She'd gone to live with Tommy in California while she was in elementary school and spent her summers and some holidays with our mother in Oklahoma. Returning a final time at the age of fourteen, Jennifer was convinced she wanted to live near her siblings and other extended Oklahoma family. The shock and worry our family experienced when she disappeared at the age of twenty was devastating, especially for Mom and Tommy. She was his *only* child, and he'd followed every possible lead in his search for her. We were crushed because the result of all the searching ended with her death. Between talking to the police and contacting friends and relatives, Tommy was constantly on the move. We all functioned as if we were comatose, barely eating and catching bits of sleep here and there. We were hurt and suffering, needing relief for an injury only God could heal. While working at a local hospital as an administrative assistant, I found myself crying often. It was a personal battle struggling with the grief while trying to pretend things were okay. I knew I'd have a few days off for Jenny's funeral but felt I needed a much longer time to deal with the shock and pain. I was a robot, mechanically answering phones and handling my office duties as efficiently as possible. Thank heavens for my coworkers who remained the greatest support I could have imagined. Being caring and concerned, they frequently checked in on me to make sure I was okay. I knew they must have noticed the circles under my eyes and the grief I wore daily as part of my office apparel.

My sister Jackie also worked while functioning as a primary caretaker of Jennifer's two small daughters (Katie and Emma) along with my mother. Since Mom and Jackie lived together, sharing expenses and the care of the girls, it proved to be a good arrangement. With both of them under school age, I was thankful Mom didn't work outside of the home. That helped!

I thought often about Jenny's life and her search for her place in this world. Though she was happy being back with Mom and the rest of her Oklahoma family once she moved from California, her focus on school dwindled, and eventually, she lost all interest in attending high school. She eventually met and fell in love with the man she believed she'd marry, Jake. And though the couple seemed very happy for a time, their relationship lasted only a few years.

A week passed (after I'd seen Jennifer's reconstructed likeness on TV), and we drove to the police station to see her privately. It was shocking! Since Jackie had Jenny's daughters with her, Tommy, Mom, and I went alone to see Jenny, or what we were allowed to see of her. In a word, it was surreal. My crying jags came and went, never helping me feel any better, only emptier. The days since I'd first seen her likeness on TV, August third, were the hardest I'd ever endured. I constantly wondered how other families cope and simply survive when someone they love is murdered. There were no easy answers. Investigators identified Jennifer through dental records the day after I saw her on TV. However, our family wasn't officially notified it was her until August seventh. We heard the gruesome truth then. She'd been stabbed in her head multiple times and had her throat cut. Her killer then decided to try and hide the crime by burning her body, reducing her to a nameless victim. I felt numb, incredibly shocked *anyone* could do what her killer did.

Slowly and quietly, we walked into the "visiting" room. Her reconstructed head was placed on a table, face forward toward the door as if she were expecting us. But she showed no emotion, of course, just the blank lifeless stare I'd seen on TV the previous week. The three of us cried, talking to her and telling her how much we loved and missed her. How could this be Jennifer? We touched her, wishing she could feel the caresses meant to comfort and assure her we were there. It helped to be near her, but this wasn't the Jennifer we'd known. It was only a part, a cold clay imitation, and we were keenly aware of the stark difference. Despite the fact she had a different dad, I loved her as if she'd been my full-blood sister. And I still do. She was my little "sissy." I wished with all of my heart I could bring her back. Twenty-six years younger than me, it wasn't fair she was dead. Period.

I thought back to the first time I'd ever seen her, only a few hours old, wriggling and squirming in her hospital incubator. The thick black curly hair was incredible. She'd looked like a live doll with lots of hair, only animated! The whole family fell in love with her, especially her four sisters and two brothers. What we saw at the police station was only a replica of who she'd been. But at least it was enough...enough to recognize a small part of our Jennifer.

Tommy looked tired and restless, moving out of sheer anxiety and pacing within the small room. He especially wasn't eating well or getting much sleep. And Mom, she just looked like she would cry at any moment, without notice.

"The forensic detective did a great job considering what she had to work with, didn't she?" one of us noted.

We all agreed the reconstruction was incredible! The police artist, Traci, had no real likeness to work with since Jennifer was burned well beyond recognition. One by one, we gently touched her for what would be our last time.

I remembered back a few months ago to the time when God "showed" me that Jennifer was dead. I'd prayed day after day and night after night since her disappearance the previous December 2005, "Dear Lord, please just let me know if she's alive or dead." One of our fears was possible kidnapping or even torture. But we held on to the hope she was still alive...*somewhere.*

My prayer was answered in February 2006, a couple of months after her disappearance (which was six months before I saw her reconstruction on TV). God did show me in an incredibly amazing way, he *had* Jennifer and she was gone from this life. I'd fallen asleep at the end of the usual work day, asking God as I dozed off, to answer my prayer. Did he ever! And I'll never forget the joy, pain, and peace which overwhelmed me while having the "reunion" with Jenny in my sleep! What an amazing experience!

In the dream, my mother, three living sisters, and I were seated around a large brown, oval-shaped dining room table. Mom sat at the head of the table with my sister Kim at the opposite end. Connie and Jackie were talking with Kim, and I sat across from them, looking at my mother. I watched as Mom's fifth and youngest daughter, Jennifer, stood between Mom and my sister Jackie. Strangely, I noticed my two brothers weren't there. (Perhaps this was because they both lived out of town, away from the rest of us). Focusing on her appearance, I noticed Jennifer appeared to be about ten years old and was dressed in a glowing white dress. She stood facing Mom, tapping her shoulder and trying to get her attention, saying, "Momma, Mommy, Mom…" Obviously, my mother didn't see her, nor did any of my other sisters. They continued talking among themselves, my mother listening to them but not speaking. I looked at my mother and then at Jennifer. I just couldn't understand why Mom was ignoring her, but I was ecstatic she was there. Then Jenny looked straight at me and *realized I could see her!* She looked surprised, relief and joy spreading across her face. I stood up quickly, moving around the table toward her, my heart beating like a drum. She had an incredible brightness surrounding her, as if she emitted the light herself! Running toward each other, we embraced, hugging each other tightly. I felt the tears flow down my face and was nearly blinded by the intensity of her glow! And her smile was dazzling! I'd never seen her so happy!

"Jennifer, I miss you and I love you so much! We *all* love you so much," I blurted out loudly between sobs. "I'm so sorry..." I heard myself say. I realized at the moment she hugged me, she was dead, physically. Gone.

She ignored my apology regarding her death and simply asked, "Yes, but you love my girls, right?" She asked this exact question three times in a row, smiling the whole time. Her face beamed, happy to hear me say I loved them.

"Yes Jennifer, I love your girls, but not just because they're Emma and Katie. I love them because they're a part of you," I answered, somewhat impatiently. I just wanted to tell her I loved *her* and missed *her*. She, however, was just concerned about her girls. It was all she wanted to say.

She didn't discuss them further; she was finished. My Technicolor dream was over, and she'd relayed the message she wanted to give. She wanted to be sure I looked after her girls. Then she began to slowly fade, in a twinkling fashion, just as I'd seen in countless movies. And, just as quickly as it arrived, the dream ended.

The prayers I'd prayed to God were answered, in particular, that specific prayer, "Lord, please just let me know if she's alive or dead." I knew, really *knew* he would answer, *when the time was right*. Two and a half months after her disappearance, I knew she was with God.

Jolted awake and highly emotional, I looked at my bedside clock. It was 11:00 p.m., on the nose. I couldn't believe it. The entire dream took place between ten thirty and eleven! I knew this because I watched all of the ten o'clock news, which ended at 10:30 p.m.

Not wanting the dream to be true but realizing it was, I cried out, "She's dead!" repeatedly while wailing into my pillow. "God, thank you for letting me see my sister one more time!" I heard myself cry out, next.

I was so thankful! The stab in my heart was unbearable, and I couldn't imagine her not coming back. But God allowed me to see my little sister once more. I couldn't help wondering why she'd looked so young though. Was it because of what Jesus taught about not being able to enter the kingdom of heaven unless you change and become like little children? I didn't understand exactly *what* just took place, but I knew it hadn't been a mere dream. I actually saw her, touched her, and *talked* to her! She was smiling, happy and glowing, in fact. I'd never seen her so peaceful, and I wanted her to be happy. I just didn't want her to be gone. Still, it was incredible the way God answered my prayer…My first prayer (regarding our loss of Jennifer) was answered!

I couldn't sleep, so I got up, pacing and wandering through the house thinking, *How would I break this to Mom?* I couldn't imagine myself telling her Jenny was dead.

A fleeting image of Jennifer flashed through my mind, a memory of Jenny at the bowling alley with several family members when she was about the same age as in my dream. Her long sun-kissed brown hair whipped around her face as she ran to pick out her bowling ball, and her green, almond-shaped eyes sparkled with excitement, those lovely green eyes that looked much like my own. Out of the seven children Mom had, Jenny and I both thought it was so cool being the only two green-eyed kids.

Confidently, she giggled as she struggled to pick up the heavy bowling ball she'd chosen. "Hey, Momma, look at me! I can pick this up by myself!" she bragged, in her high-pitched Betty Boop voice. "Watch me get a strike!" Her youthful voice was etched into my memory. Staggering under the weight of the heavy ball, she approached the lane. Step, step, *thud!* She dropped the ball, and we all watched as it slowly rolled toward the edge of the lane, wobbling and finally landing in the gutter. She didn't care! She'd laughed, wanting to do it again, smiling and pushing up her little plastic frame glasses that slid down her nose. I hope and pray I never forget her youthful little voice, the innocent little girl I remembered who had so much enthusiasm, so much happy energetic *life* within her bursting to get out.

Bowling with Jenny

How comforted I was when I remembered (years ago) my mom telling me Jennifer had become a Christian. And I knew she'd accepted Christ as her Savior because of things she'd written in her Bible. Had she been perfect? No. None of us are. But knowing she'd had a relationship with the Lord took some of the sting out of her death. She'd written actual prayers in the back of her Bible, short and intimate ones. I knew she was a believer but didn't know how much it meant until I read the notes.

God, thank you for letting me see my little sister one more time, I thought again, silently. *Please tell her I love her and I wish she were here.*

Finally settling back into bed for the rest of the night, I wondered about telling my mom Jennifer wasn't coming back alive. I talked to God, asking him to guide me in breaking the news to her. I knew it would be the worst day of her life! I also knew there'd be a lot of people praying for some kind of information regarding Jenny's disappearance. Everyone would want answers and pray for God to show us where she was located. Did someone bury her in a shallow grave somewhere? Was she in a different state?

For months after her disappearance, everyone we knew prayed for Jennifer's return. One of those people who prayed was my own father who lives in Colorado. He was dedicated to praying for her, calling me frequently and asking if we'd heard anything about Jennifer. Always I'd had to tell him the same thing, "No, not yet."

I never dreamed the young lady shown on TV in December of 2005, who'd been discovered burning in a field and described by the media as possibly being of Asian descent, could be our own Jennifer. The drawn sketch of what authorities believed the burned young woman looked like bore little resemblance to her. I remember sitting down, covering a gasp with my hand, and saying, “Oh that poor family!” My eyes filled with tears as I looked at the young woman, so young…now dead. I felt a flood of compassionate concern for the girl’s family. Of course it never crossed my mind it could be *our* lost one, and we were the “poor family” who would receive the horrible news at some point. When the picture was shown on television, we didn’t want to even believe Jenny was truly missing. We were in denial, trying to convince ourselves she’d been out of contact with the family because she was occupied with her new boyfriend.

The month after my dream “visit” from Jenny, my own father called. I couldn’t believe it was March and there was no new info about her disappearance. I’d already tried to tell my mom about the dream of seeing Jennifer, but she didn’t want to hear Jenny could be dead. She held out hope until the day detectives confirmed it was Jenny’s body they’d identified. However, my dad had a special dream too and wanted to share it with me.

“Honey, I had a dream about Jennifer. In the dream it seemed like she was cold,” he said.

“What do you mean, Dad? Like out in some old broken-down structure in some cold remote location or something?”

“I don’t know,” he answered. “I just know she’s cold.”

We would find out many months later, he was right. Her body *was* cold. Her skeletal remains were located at the medical examiner’s office, presumably stored and waiting for a family to claim them. I’d told my dad the previous month about her “visit” to me when I first realized she was dead. So it didn't surprise me he kept praying, hoping for answers to where her body was located. I believed what he'd told me since Dad has also dreamed of loved ones who've passed on. He was almost as anxious as I was to find her! Looking back on all we'd been through, we were just grateful to be getting her body back, even in its sad condition.

Turning my focus to the rubber hair on Jenny's reconstruction, I couldn't help but remember her real hair. The killer destroyed all of that too. She'd had gorgeous hair most of her life. It was *all* only a memory now, nothing left but her bones.

Our short visit with Jennifer came to an end, and we reluctantly told her good-bye. My legs felt like they had a will of their own, with no desire to carry my body down the hallway toward the police station exit door. I wanted to stay with Jennifer but knew I couldn't. I knew we all wanted to.

"Thanks for letting us spend some time with Jenny today," Tommy told the police officer who passed by us as we approached the door to leave. I remembered he escorted us to her visiting room on our way in.

"No problem! You guys take care," he said sympathetically as he glanced toward Mom, who was still wiping tears from her eyes.

A harsh gust of blistering Oklahoma heat blew through the door as Tommy pushed it open. Without a word, I knew we were all thinking the same thing as we walked toward the car. Today was our *last* glimpse of Jennifer in this lifetime.

GRIEF AND MEMORIES

"I can't believe it's taking so long to get her body back," Tommy stated impatiently time and again. "The authorities have had her body for eight months, and I just want to get her back and get on with the funeral." He looked sad, lost, and bewildered. He'd lost weight he really couldn't afford to lose. Looking shell shocked, he spoke softly, as if the grief in his soul had moved in for good, kicking out the spunk and energy that made him Tommy. He reminded me of a man who had been punched in the stomach eight months ago and still couldn't catch his breath. He paced constantly, listening to his iPod. His friend Robert Burgeis had written a song as a tribute to Jennifer, a song many of us listened to repeatedly, finding comfort in the thought she was (as the song said) "where there's no pain." He named the song "Promiseland—Jenny's Song," and we planned to have it played at her funeral.

As hard as it was for me to absorb what happened, I couldn't imagine being in Tommy's or Mom's shoes. Since her body was burned to destroy evidence, the police had to identify Jennifer through dental records, a *constant* reminder of just how badly her body was burned. This work proved to be a quick process, so we couldn't understand why her body wasn't released to the funeral home more quickly. Our frustration mounted, the extreme August heat fraying the edges of our nerves a little more with each day while we were forced to wait for her return to our family.

"At least we have a funeral to prepare now. Thank the Lord for that!" I pointed out. "Remember when you came to Oklahoma back in January looking for her, Tommy? At least we don't have to wonder where she is for the rest of our lives now," I pointed out wistfully. I knew Mom and Tommy were thankful they'd get to bury their daughter, but it hurt them horribly. They just couldn't believe their hopes of having her back alive were ended. Looking into their eyes was sometimes more than I could handle. How does someone comfort another when you can't fully imagine their pain? How can one comfort another when you can't even comfort yourself?

Mom dealt with her loss in her own way. She slept. At times she had to use sleeping pills because she couldn't truly rest, and no one could blame her! My heart was torn, watching her sleep then seeing her awaken each day to start crying all over again. She was an endless well of tears. She tried hiding it, of course, staying in her bedroom much of the time, emerging only for a meal or to spend a few moments with Jenny's little girls.

"Who killed her? And how did the attack take place?" we continuously asked ourselves that same thought, angrily. We couldn't imagine who would attack a one-hundred-pound female of her small stature, or why the attack was so vicious. I wanted to see her, the *real* her, hug her, and hear her voice. How I wanted to hear her call me sissy just once more. In fact, I found myself wanting to hear her say anything again. I thought of the silly voice mail recordings she'd put on my mom's phone and how Mom had scolded her for changing them from the typical, "Please leave a message and I'll call you back" recording. I'd love to hear her nutty messages now. I actually had prayed to God to help me locate an old answering machine that I was certain had a cassette tape in it with her voice on it, requesting I call her back or answer the phone. But I couldn't find it. Whether I'd thrown it out or given it away, I didn't have it any longer. But I had other memories too, memories of her as a young mother trying her best to comfort and care for her children when they were tiny. A quick flashback of one particularly desperate phone call from her crossed my mind.

"Hello?" I answered as the phone rang one afternoon.

"Hey, sis, it's me, Jennifer! Can you come over here and help me with Katie? I can't get her to stop crying," she frantically begged. "She doesn't like me. No matter what I do, she just cries!" She sounded so stressed, her high-pitched words spilled out quickly.

"All right, all right, calm down. I'll be over in just a few minutes, okay? It'll be all right," I assured her while hearing Katie cry loudly in the background. "Just hold her and talk to her until I get there. Or sing to her and see if that helps," I offered.

"Okay, thanks! And please hurry!" I heard the instant relief in her voice just before she hung up, and I couldn't wait to get to her place and help her.

I pulled into her driveway and ran up the stairs to the porch. Swinging the front door open, I quickly walked to her bedroom where Jenny sat on the edge of the bed, crying. Katie lay nearby, screaming and kicking her tiny legs, red faced and very upset. As I picked her newborn baby up, I moved close to Jennifer and put my arm around her shoulder, trying to comfort her too.

"You know, it's okay to ask for help, hon. New moms *have* to have help sometimes. It doesn't mean you're a bad mom," I advised. And then slowly, a tiny smile lit up her face, and I could tell she'd be okay. Carefully, I handed Katie to her, and she gave her baby a little kiss.

The sound of Mom's voice brought me back to the present, and I heard the anger she couldn't contain. "I just hope and pray the police find whoever did this to her so they can't do it again to somebody else's daughter!" She wiped her eyes with a tissue and continued, "I just hope they find them soon! And whoever did it needs to have someone do exactly the same to them as they did to Jennifer!" She called the phantom murderer several choice names, names I wasn't sure she's ever even heard before. I've never seen her so desperate and angry! She was inconsolable, absolutely gut-wrenchingly heartbroken. If she hadn't thought the neighbors would call the police, I knew she'd have screamed her lungs out, day after day, like a crazed woman confined in a home for the mentally ill. She didn't though...somehow, she held it together.

The detectives were in touch, checking every possible lead in my sister's murder. Every tiny piece of information was checked; anyone even slightly suspicious was considered as a possible link to finding Jenny's killer. All roads led nowhere. But we were hopeful, I was *extremely* hopeful. I believed. I truly believed clues would fall into place. Somehow the killer would trip himself or herself up. I believed *somehow* our case would have a conclusion, something we could live with. I didn't know how it would come about, but I knew I could pray about it, asking again for God to show me what happened, how the attack occurred or even who her killer was. As it happened, God revealed even more than I had prayed for. He even delivered it with incredible timing.

Then it happened, finally the day we'd waited for. We were notified Jennifer's body was being transported to a funeral home of our choosing, and we could visit her remains along with friends and extended family. We decided to bury Jennifer on August 28, 2006. And we knew her skeletal remains were all we'd be burying. We tried not to focus on this fact and reminded ourselves she would at least have a face. The forensic artist had been able to arrange for Jenny to keep the reconstruction, and we were overjoyed! It was one small kindness shown to our family meaning more than words could ever express. The normal routine with such a reconstruction was to remove it before burial because of its expensive components. For our family, they made an exception. The forensic police artist will forever have our thanks, and we hope she can help other families as she's helped ours.

We knew even though much had been taken from Jennifer's body, we wanted to bury her in an adult-sized casket, far larger than she would need but appropriate just the same. She would have no open-casket viewing, of course. What a stab to the heart! Most families could see their loved one once more before burial, but *not ours*. Most would get to reach out and smooth their clothing, brush their fingers across their beloved's skin one last time. *We couldn't*. Many even give a final kiss on the forehead. *We could not*. We could only visualize the casket contents… bones, and nothing more.

I thought of the last time I'd seen her. How I wish I'd known it was to be my last! She was clowning around with my sister Connie at Mom's house, making goofy faces, and laughing. It was the perfect time to have my camera available. Holding up their glasses of iced tea, they teasingly threatened to soak each other. "Say cheese," I ordered. They obeyed, sitting down side by side on the couch, putting their heads together. "Cheese!" they blurted out simultaneously. Dressed in a red tank top shirt and jeans, Jenny posed, giggling. Her dark brown hair was tousled, and she wore the wire-framed glasses she occasionally misplaced.

Connie and Jennifer, 2005

The cold pink metal casket beautifully displayed the quilt spread across the top. *Jennifer* had been embroidered in the center of the quilt along with her date of birth and death. It was just so sobering! I ran my finger across her name, saying it out loud, slowly, not wanting her name to be forgotten. I wanted her name to be spoken every day for the rest of my life, as if she were still here. I couldn't bear the thought of it fading from our conversations. I knew I couldn't let that happen. No matter how much it hurt, I promised myself I'd always say her name…many times a day.

Flowers of every color and variety arrived at the funeral home. Soft pink azaleas were placed near a large photo of Jennifer's smiling face. Other multiple arrangements stood near the head and foot of her casket, brightening their intended location with deep purples and several shades of pink we knew she would have loved. Visitors filed in, signing her guestbook and offering condolences. I paced, looking at the quilt and flowers, occasionally whispering to my best friend, Sheila, who had flown in for the funeral. The sadness was a dull ache. No one wanted to say good-bye…

I looked at another picture of her, placed on a table near her casket, and remembered her wearing the dress in the photo when she was a small girl. A deep velvet blue dress with a white ruffle lace collar made her look so petite and girlish, a beautiful child! Yet she was just as comfortable running in torn jeans and tennis shoes. Her impish four-year-old smile could melt a heart. And she did, many times. I wiped a tear and sat down, thinking of how very beautiful her viewing room looked. I knew she would have loved it and that she would be greatly missed by many.

Jennifer's viewing room, abundant with beautiful flowers

The funeral service itself was a blur, but I knew August 28, 2006, was a date I'd never forget...Jenny's burial date. She was killed during an exceedingly cold night and was buried on an extremely hot summer day. Extremes! So many things about her murder seemed extreme or strangely notable.

The minister spoke, trying to bring comfort to our family, remarking on Jennifer's eternal rest and peace with our Lord Jesus Christ. He then unfolded the piece of paper I'd given to him to share with the congregation. It was a tribute I'd written to Jenny regarding her life and our fond memories of her. It was amazingly comforting, hearing him read my notes about teaching her to roller blade. And he laughed briefly when he read the part about her "Urkel" impression, an imitation she'd perfected from a '90s TV sitcom. (Bickley, & Warren)[1] She'd pull her jeans up to her chest and deliver Urkel's trademark catchphrase while whining in her best nasally voice, "Did I do thaat?" (Bickley, & Warren)[1] It was hilarious! She was a clown, a daughter, a mom, my sister, and she was gone.

I wiped at more tears, glancing at my sister Kim who sat next to me. She burst out crying, leaning her head toward mine. "I mmmiss her sssoo much!" she wailed. I'd never heard her cry this way before. She wanted someone to make it better, but I couldn't. I wanted to. I really *tried.* I simply couldn't.

"Kim, it will be okay. She's not hurting now," I whispered softly.

Hands shaking, she handed pictures to me while we sat there on the church pew looking at Jenny's casket. They were pictures of Jennifer, as a child, she'd rummaged around for and found at home. She wanted them put into the casket with Jenny. I told her we'd have to have someone else put them inside since we weren't allowed to open the casket. Jennifer's adolescence had been tough, I knew, like most teens. She'd been searching for her own identity, rebelling against authority, at times, wanting to follow her own path. She simply wanted to grow up. But the pictures Kim held now showed the little fireball we had all loved and remembered.

I knew Kim was having an extremely hard time dealing with Jennifer's death, remembering the small child she'd been once and the woman she'd grown to be. And I thought of Jenny's last birthday, her twentieth, not

---

[1] 'Bickley, William, & Warren , Michael, Family Matters, TV'

realizing it would be her last one. I'd teased her while she cooked some lunch in Mom's kitchen.

"Happy birthday, sis! How does it feel to not be a teenager anymore?" I'd questioned her. "Now you're an old fogey like the rest of us...ha ha ha!" I laughed.

"I don't feel any different!" she defended herself, in a matter-of-fact tone. I could tell she knew I was trying to push a button. She wasn't falling for it though and asked if I wanted lunch.

"No, you go ahead and have some, birthday girl. I'm waiting for the cake!" I answered with a big smile that said I wouldn't tease her anymore. I had no idea it would be my last chance to ever give her a birthday hug. No more birthdays with Jennifer. No more teasing with her. No more time with her.

The music brought me back and struck everyone's emotions, bringing the congregation to the realization a young, beautiful, vivacious woman had been savagely struck down in the prime of her life, leaving two little girls to go on without her. Mom shook her head, crying as if the service were surely just a bad dream. Tommy sat silently, resolved one moment, shoulders shaking with sobs the next. "When I Get Where I'm Going" (written by George Teren and Rivers Rutherford) gently flowed through the airwaves of the chapel. The song (performed by Brad Paisley and Dolly Parton) told of a person looking forward to seeing a beloved grandfather who'd already passed on to heaven, and mentions the anticipation of walking with him again.

The sad, beautiful song was a reminder that Jennifer would meet loved ones who've passed before, in particular, her famous grandfather, Leonard Sipes. Most people remember him by his "stage" name of Tommy Collins. A talented singer-songwriter of country/western music, he wrote and performed an incredible list of songs. Creating his own unique style of music, he changed the sound of country throughout the '50s, '60s, and '70s. Some of those hits included "You Better Not Do That," and "If You Can't Bite Don't Growl." He also wrote songs which were performed by other artists and became big hits, such as "If You Ain't Lovin' You Ain't Livin" (performed by George Strait), "New Patches" (performed by Mel Tillis), and "Carolyn" (performed by Merle Haggard). There was even a tribute song written *for* Tommy Collins by Merle Haggard called "Leonard." An awesome story within a song, it mentions Leonard's rise to fame and his struggle for personal and spiritual fulfillment along the road to following his dream. I remembered Jenny also shared his love of music. In fact, she loved singing and had a very beautiful voice.

Along with other family who've passed on, I believed she was with her grandfather from the moment she died. And a little known fact is that she was being buried in the *very* spot originally meant for him. Living in Tennessee during the later years of his life, he was buried there, away from his Oklahoma roots. However, it worked out perfectly for Jennifer to be laid to rest in the location initially reserved for him. I was comforted by just knowing she'd be buried in Oklahoma City where I could visit her grave regularly. I sniffled and blew my nose, feeling the beginnings of a headache appear.

"Focus on the funeral!" I scolded myself.

I thought of my two adult sons both living in Texas and wished they were here. But life had drawn both of them to colleges and futures away from home. The timing was just rotten and neither could make it home for the funeral. They had no choice but to grieve in their own way from a distance. As "Promiseland—Jenny's Song" drifted throughout the chapel, fresh tears welled up inside me.

Promiseland—Jenny's Song

I say good-bye to my little girl today. The Lord came and took her away
And though it hurt and tears filled my eyes, I heard a voice say "Son, don't cry.
Don't cry...
She's where the blind all see and crippled walk on brand-new feet,
Where there's no pain and the grass is green and it never rains.
Where the streets are paved with gold...and it's never, ever cold.
Tonight with Jesus she stands...in the promised land."

Too many times we forget our lives are so delicate.
But just remember with a little faith, we'll meet again in that heavenly place...
Heavenly place...
Where the blind all see where the crippled walk on brand new feet,
Where there's no pain where the grass is green and it never rains.
The streets are paved with gold...and it's never, ever cold.
Tonight with Jesus she stands...in the promised land.

> So lift your head up towards the sky, 'cause tonight
> she's in paradise
> Where the blind all see where the crippled walk
> on brand-new feet
> Where there's no pain where the grass is green
> and it never rains.
> Where the streets are paved with gold and it's
> never, ever cold.
> Tonight with Jesus she stands in the promised land...
> Tonight with Jesus she stands in the promised
> land...the promised land...
>
> —Robert Burgeis

The words appeared to touch the entire crowd. Someone patted my shoulder from the bench behind me. Then the person sniffled and choked up, saying, "It's okay." I looked around once more and noticed there didn't appear to be a dry eye in the room.

All of Jennifer's dreams, her hopes, her plans were being buried today, along with her body. Those dreams of getting her GED...gone! Her goal of attending the local community college...gone! Taking the walk down the aisle to get that coveted associates degree...gone!

She'd wanted it so badly and talked about it often, a few years earlier, when she knew I was taking a couple of courses there myself to complete a degree I was pursuing.

"You really think I could get a degree there too?" she'd asked once during a conversation we'd had.

"Of course! You're a smart girl. You just have to focus and keep going. You know...stay determined. The hardest part is just walking through the door and getting enrolled.

You'll ace the GED test *first* though because I'll help you study," I encouraged her, with a cocky grin.

"No, I'll ace the test because I'm *smart*!" she quickly fired back with a defensive tone, flashing her eyes at me.

"That's the attitude! And don't forget it!" I jokingly ordered.

"Okay, bossy!" she volleyed back loudly.

Her competitive nature erupted, reminding me she'd always possessed the attitude of a little banty rooster when challenged. We could've gone on for hours, each trying to have the "last word," but I knew better than to keep going down *that* road with her. Jennifer would win. She hated giving in on an argument.

The service was over, and I stood to follow my family outdoors toward the hearse. Straining to look back once more toward Jennifer's pictures, I stumbled.

Pay attention and keep moving, I silently ordered myself.

Somewhere I'd heard before that our God doesn't give us more than we can bear. But I knew it wasn't his will that Jennifer was dead. God did *not* give us this cross to bear. He was not responsible for what had happened to Jennifer. Someone in our society was, possibly even someone in our city.

I let my thoughts wander down the same road they always seemed to go down, wondering who the responsible person or people were. Then I imagined her fighting for her life.

HOW DID THE ATTACK HAPPEN?

September arrived, and with it came the realization Tommy just couldn't stay in Oklahoma any longer. The funeral was over, and I was facing a new month with both sadness and relief. We'd buried Jenny, and it was time to get on with our lives, as empty as they seemed.

"Okay, you girls be good for Grandma and Aunt Jackie," Tommy advised, in the most lighthearted voice he could muster, hugging Katie and Emma good-bye. "I'll be back sometime soon, maybe even before Christmas, and we'll go pick out your Christmas presents together." I could tell he didn't want to leave them. I noticed the gleam in the girls' eyes when they heard *that* important bit of news. They seemed to hug his neck just a little bit tighter. Katie, at the ripe old age of four and half years, knew Christmas meant new toys for her and her three-year-old sister. And they both believed you couldn't have too many toys!

Tommy left, walking out to the rental car he would drive to the airport. Jenny's burial had taken place only a few days earlier, and we knew Tommy needed to return to California, to his own home. After all, he had doctor appointments, other friends and family, and his little dog waiting for him there. Life and our normal routines had to resume. My best friend, Sheila, went home also to Florida and to her waiting family. What a blessing to have someone so caring and compassionate as she was to leave her family and be by my side during the worst event of my life. God had blessed me with the best buddy I could have ever asked for, and I knew I'd miss her company after she'd gone home.

As September passed by, each day felt like a repeat of the previous day. Get up, go to work, pretend everything is okay, cry a few times, and go home. It was all I had to look forward to for the next several months. I had to get beyond the grief and disbelief of what happened to Jennifer. But something wonderful happened while I sat at my desk, struggling to stay on task.

A lady I'd recently met through work came into our department and asked why I looked so sad.

"Are you okay?" she wanted to know.

The fatigue and sadness I felt were constant companions, and just about everyone noticed. Realizing she didn't know about my sister's murder, I briefly explained our family's loss, and she gave me the number of a grief counselor she knew through a local hospice organization. It was exactly what I needed and I knew it.

After visiting briefly on the phone, we arranged a date and time for him to visit with our family. We were thrilled! Actually, *I* was thrilled, and my mother reluctantly agreed. She wasn't up to seeing anyone and didn't really want a stranger coming into her home. She didn't think he could relate to her because he probably didn't have a murdered daughter, etc., etc. Excuse after excuse, she wasn't comfortable going in to a counselor's office for help, nor was she interested in having one come to her. Finally, I convinced her, and the counselor (Mr. Willis) graciously came to my mom's home, bringing paperwork-type "tools" designed to help us deal with the grief. The compassionate assistance he gave was invaluable, especially the information regarding the normal responses to grief and loss. I would refer to the list of responses many times, reassuring my mom she wasn't going crazy. She was normal.

"But why don't I dream about her?" she'd cry.

I couldn't answer her. She'd hoped to dream about Jenny, to be able to tell her good-bye and how she loved her, anything. But a dream didn't come. There aren't always answers, and this is the hardest part of helping someone who is grieving. I was finding out the hard way.

Mr. Willis was not only helpful in getting our family started in healing our hearts, he was also planning to speak at a homicide survivor seminar the following month and put me in contact with the homicide advocate within the district attorney's office so I could arrange to attend the seminar. It was scheduled for October 12, 2006, and both Mom and I eagerly accepted the invitation we received to attend. Hoping for information regarding the investigation process and justice system in Oklahoma, we arrived with our notepad and pens. We were also told we could bring a picture of Jenny to show the other families at the seminar and had decided to bring one of her large photos we'd displayed at her funeral. We were grateful to be there, learning and asking questions along with the others who'd lost someone to murder.

Lunchtime arrived, and we sat silently, enjoying the food provided for us while looking through some of the handouts from the seminar. My eyes were drawn to a baby blue sheet toward the back of the handouts. It stated there was to be an observation called "Tree of Honor and Remembrance," to be held toward the end of November in Oklahoma City, and I made a mental note to tell Tommy about the event in case he wanted to fly back to attend it. The paper said families could bring a Christmas tree ornament in honor of their family member who was a victim of a violent crime. I imagined decorating an ornament with Jenny's name on it and adding it to one of those trees.

Jenny, we're going to get you one of those, I thought, showing the paper to Mom. I knew Jennifer would have loved the idea.

The drive home was quiet, both Mom and myself lost within our own thoughts. I knew she was trying to absorb all she'd heard at the seminar earlier, and I thought again how miraculous it was we were even able to bury our loved one. After all, so many people came up missing and were never found. I couldn't imagine how their families coped with having no body for burial! I remembered those eight agonizing long months and Mom mentioning every so often we could try contacting a psychic to tell us where Jennifer was and even what happened to her. Always, I told her the same thing. "Mom, we just need to have a little trust in God. He *will* come through and let us know when *he* is ready and thinks *we're* ready to hear it. Don't give in and do it. I've read several places in the Bible we're supposed to put our faith in God and nothing else. We just have to have faith, Mom. We have to be patient."

I remember thinking (during her disappearance) maybe God didn't *want* us to know immediately what happened because he knew we couldn't handle the news, whatever it turned out to be. Maybe we had to have some time without her first in order for us to hear the painful news of her murder. It was so hard for Mom to wait and for all of us too. I distinctly remember feeling God would come through and answer our prayers about Jennifer, just as he allowed the dream that gave me a chance to tell her good-bye. I felt good knowing, for probably the first time in my life, I was learning *true faith* in God answering a prayer! It was a very empowering faith-building feeling. And to really believe he would answer my prayer plus let me feel being truly loved was incredible!

Time dragged on, the month of October slowly arriving and bringing with it the sadness of knowing Jennifer would never experience another one. No Thanksgiving. No Christmas. In fact, it would be our second Christmas without her. I thought of Jenny's love of the holidays as I noticed the leaves turning, their magical assortment of colors decorating the trees throughout my neighborhood and much of Oklahoma. How could there be so much gold, red, purple, and green still left in the world when our lives felt so gray? Everywhere I looked, bright orange pumpkins filled the landscape, spreading their fall "cheer" as they sat plump and ripe in my neighbors' yards. I love autumn and normally enjoy nature's brilliant display of colors, but this year, I felt a deep sadness Jenny would never experience another one. The guilt of simply being alive to *see* the brilliance of fall when she could *not* was overwhelming! I knew I had a lot to be thankful for this Thanksgiving but still felt the hot sting of tears burn my eyes as I looked at all she'd never see again. How unfair it seemed. How final!

My mind was saturated with thoughts of my little sister. I found myself dreaming of her while I slept often. They were normal dreams, dreams of our family looking for her still, as if we'd never found her. Dream after dream, we'd come close to having her back, but just as we'd see her, she'd turn a corner and slip away. Or she'd tell us she was coming home and then vanish before our eyes. The frustration and disappointment was overwhelming!

My waking hours were filled with questions. Exactly what happened to her the day she died? How on earth could this happen? I couldn't turn off the questions in my mind. I constantly talked to God, wanting to know more, pleading with him for more answers. Thankfully, he was listening to my prayers, as I soon found out. On October 22, 2006, I had my *second* dream, which gave clues to what happened to Jennifer! The answer to prayer number three unfolded:

The dream began with me walking into my mother's home, looking for Jennifer.

"Where is she?" I asked Mom as I went into her kitchen.

"In my bedroom, sleeping," she replied.

I approached her bedroom, noticing the darkness and the still quiet of the room. I felt suddenly overwhelmed with sadness as I looked at Jennifer lying on the floor on a pallet, blankets spread upon the floor below and on top of her. I remember thinking, in the dream, how really odd that she wasn't asleep on the bed. Kneeling near her, I touched her shoulder, trying to wake her up.

"Jennifer? Wake up," I told her, shaking her shoulder a little more roughly.

"What?" she mumbled softly as she tried to open her eyes.

"Jennifer, can I pray for you?" I asked while she rubbed her eyes, trying to focus on my face.

"Yeah," she said, nodding off to sleep again, as if she just couldn't stay awake.

I briefly uttered a small prayer for her and gave her a quick hug. Then the dream ended, and I woke up. It was just that fast! What a short, insignificant dream I thought I'd had. As it turned out, it was another piece of the puzzle to Jennifer's murder. And as I would come to find out in the following months, it fit perfectly with the story her killer would give. How amazing God truly is! I was finding this new at every turn in Jenny's story. He was answering my prayers, giving me information along the way—in this instance, a clue as to what happened. Of course, I thought it was just plain weird I had a dream about someone sleeping. I'd never had dreams of this kind before. It definitely was a first! And she was so very out of it like she couldn't wake up. As we would come to find out later, the killer would admit he attacked her with a baseball bat *while she slept*. So my prayer of, *Lord, what happened to her the day she died?* was not overlooked. I counted them off in my mind realizing prayer number three was answered. God revealed what she'd been doing at the moment she was attacked.

I told my mom about the dream the next morning, and she agreed it really was a strange one! In fact, my mom and my aunt (Mom's sister) stayed overnight with me the same night I had the dream, and we all believed

God was contacting us with that information because we were all so grief-stricken. We took the dream as a positive sign he was with us, trying to help us understand what happened the day she was killed so we could cope better with her death. We were encouraged again, but what we really wanted next was the killer's name and his capture. We were closer to having this prayer answered than we could imagine!

THE CONFESSION

The hustle and bustle of the 2006 holiday season arrived! Suddenly, time sped up, and I was behind in preparing for the holidays and shopping for Christmas. Like so many other people, I did it while trying to work. I managed to gather gifts for loved ones and keep up with my own household obligations. Along with my other various duties in November, I decided to attend my first homicide support group meeting held at the district attorney's victim/witness center. My first night to attend arrived, and I looked forward to the meeting. I slowly walked in, noticing there were a lot of families already there. I had no idea there could be so many broken hearts, so many families grieving in the same way we were! I took Mom with me, hoping she would benefit by visiting with a group who understood our pain. I was prepared to hear others speak of their losses, and I expected to see tears and hear the sobs of mothers, fathers, grandparents, and siblings who'd lost someone to murder. What I didn't expect was the overwhelming flood of emotions I still felt. I thought I'd dealt with Jennifer's murder *well* and was finished with the crying jags. Was I ever wrong!

I sat listening to others introduce themselves and talk about their cases. And although it helped to know others understood our pain, I also hurt for them. I heard several people mention years had gone by since their loved one was murdered. I was impressed their grief hadn't killed them. Yet I felt saddened. I couldn't believe how years later the pain could still be so intense for them! I could only wonder if my heart would be less broken a year from now as I was still struggling to get any kind of joy back into my life. I sat still, listening and absorbing their stories, imagining what their lives had been like before and after their loved one was killed.

Then after some time, I was asked if I'd like to introduce myself and mention whom I'd lost. I agreed and told the group a little about my sister and the circumstances of her disappearance. Horrible, painful emotions welled up inside me, and I felt like exploding with tears! I hurried, trying to finish my story; but before I knew it, I was blurting out the question I'd wanted to ask since I arrived.

"How do you just get through the day without feeling like you're falling apart?" I asked, sobbing loudly and looking around the room from face to face. I was a wreck and I knew it.

A particularly kind, soft-spoken gentleman answered. I remembered he had said his grandson was shot and killed several years before.

"One hour at a time. That's how you do it. Sometimes it's just one minute at a time," he said slowly. He was so soft spoken, so quiet that I strained to hear every word. His name was Ron, and I knew I'd remember his advice for many years. He seemed so wise, so seasoned in this topic of pain and yet still so hurt. And I could also tell others there looked up to him for support by the questions they asked of him that evening. How wonderful to have him in our support group, but how awful for him and his wife to have to be there. Their loss and pain was still so very obvious.

I knew, as we drove home from the meeting, I had to attend again. I also hoped someday I too could help someone else who hurt as badly as I hurt my first night there. What a great blessing to have a support group who helped others through such a hard time!

With my first homicide support group meeting behind me, I tried to imagine the upcoming Thanksgiving and what it would be like this year. I knew I had much to be thankful for but dreaded the holidays, realizing Jennifer's absence would be blatantly obvious. Regardless of how I felt, the month of November passed quickly, and before I knew it, Tommy was on his way back to Oklahoma. He arrived near Thanksgiving (November 23) in order to attend the yearly "Tree of Honor and Remembrance" observance for violent crime victims, which was to be held Tuesday, November 28, 2006. And it came as no surprise to me while we waited for the event, he threw himself back into the search for any information regarding Jenny's killer. Hour after hour he spent seeking answers, calling detectives, and trying to put together the missing pieces of Jennifer's death. I just couldn't seem to get her off my mind, either, and it seemed staying busy was the only solution for my restlessness, in fact for all of us.

Shortly after he arrived, we revisited the location where her body was found burning in the early morning hours the previous December 5, spending a few moments remembering her in the location where she lay for the very last time. The November landscape held a sparse bleakness to it; nothing but browns and grays as far as the eye could see. The area where her body had been still lacked vegetative growth as a result of the fire, which destroyed everything in its path. I could almost visualize the charred, blackened spot she left behind even though the soil had returned to a reddish clay color. I did, however, find several rocks displaying the grim reminder she'd been there. Scorched and lying near a small spindly bush, they bore testimony to the fact that something evil had taken place there, something incredibly destructive to the land and to lives, our lives. Once again, I reminded myself some selfish, psychotic individual decided to cover his dirty crime by burning Jennifer's body so she became a nameless victim while our family suffered unspeakable grief wondering where she was those eight loooong months. I stuffed one of the rocks inside the pocket of my coat, knowing it was the last thing my sister had been near. Amazingly, I felt incredibly happy at the moment I'd found it. How odd it was, one moment feeling utterly sad and the next lifted up, all because of a small rock. Still, just being there put a calming effect on me, as if she were there too in spirit. Tommy, Mom, and I stood looking at the ground and then back at each other. There was nothing to be said we hadn't said before. Mom choked back a sob, and we told Jenny we were there, as if we expected her to say something. She didn't, of course. And after a few more moments of staring silently at the ground, we left.

Thanksgiving weekend was over, and the following Monday morning arrived in a calm and deceptively normal manner. I had no idea as I drove to work this particular Monday, November 27, 2006, it would be another major life-changing day. Nonetheless, I scooted out the door, expecting my usual routine at work, which involved struggling to keep my mind off my sister and staying on task. I was excited about the upcoming ceremony the following evening and looked forward to seeing some of the people I'd met at the district attorney's office during the seminar and at the homicide support group.

Rrrring! The phones at work rang constantly, the buttons lighting up, expecting my full attention. I quickly answered a line and heard Mom's voice, asking what time the ceremony would be held the following day. Chatting briefly, I gave her the information and then the conversation turned to Tommy. Apparently, he was on the go again, heading for Edmond to talk with a detective about Jenny's case. We knew there was no new information, no new leads or suspects, yet he kept in close contact with the police, hoping for even the tiniest bit of info that might shed light on her murder. What determination he had! He was a man on a mission, but time and again, he was disappointed in the results of his pursuit. His search always seemed to lead nowhere. Maybe this time he'd learn something new. We could only hope and pray. Making my way home after work, I found Mom waiting there for me, expecting Tommy to arrive soon too. It was already after 5:00 p.m., and he'd been gone several hours, running errands and visiting with the detective.

"So how was your day, Mom? How are Katie and Emma?" I asked, hoping she'd had a stress-free day and felt well.

"Oh, it was okay," she answered mechanically. I could detect her attempt at an upbeat answer. "They're good, but Katie keeps asking why her mommy is dead. I just told her *again* a bad person hurt her and the doctors couldn't make her well. It's the same thing I always tell her. She seems to understand but keeps asking anyway. I think she just wants to talk about her," she said wistfully.

"You know it's going to be years before either of the girls really understand their mom's not coming back," I pointed out. "We just have to keep telling them the same thing. We can't give them too much information or they'll be horrified and possibly even afraid the 'bad person' will come after *them*."

"I know. You're right. We can't have them knowing too much. They don't need to start having bad dreams and worrying," she agreed, sounding tired and uninterested in talking.

I couldn't imagine the scary thoughts they might be entertaining. I visualized years of therapy down the road for Jenny's little girls. Emma was just too young to even question where her mother was. However, I could easily see her acting out and searching for answers when she entered her teen years. But Katie…she was older, more inquisitive, and she remembered her mom. She was the one who burst out crying uncontrollably when we told her Jenny was dead. I couldn't help wondering if she might actually be the one who could deal with her mother's absence and murder more easily in the future since she'd grieved along with the rest of us during the funeral period. Poor kids! I prayed our family could comfort and love them in such a way they'd grow up having peace and contentment in their lives as well as a relationship with the Lord.

The ring of the phone interrupted our conversation, and Mom quickly answered. I'm sure she was hoping for news from Tommy. And as it turned out, it *was* him.

"Where were you when you saw the family? Wow! That was nice of them!" I heard her say. Obviously she liked what he was telling her on the phone. She smiled at me while she paced throughout the living room, listening to every word Tommy told her. "Huh…well, that's nice. People don't do that too often these days," she told him after a few minutes. "Okay. We'll see you soon then. Bye," she said as she reached to hang up the phone.

"Well, it was Tommy," she said. "He's on his way here. Said he had a good visit with the detective, but there isn't anything new with the case," she stated quickly. I could hear the excitement in her voice as she rushed on to tell me what else he'd told her on the phone. "You won't believe what he said happened when he stopped at a restaurant to get breakfast in Edmond this morning on his way to the police department," she relayed. "He went into *Jimmy's Egg* and was drinking coffee about nine thirty this morning when he noticed a family a few tables away from him who were praying over their meal together. As he left the restaurant, he stopped by their table and told them he noticed them praying as a family and that he thought it was nice to see people still doing that. At some point in the conversation he mentioned Jennifer, and that he was going to talk to the detective about her unsolved case. And then they asked if he'd mind them saying a prayer right then and there for her killer to be caught. Isn't that awesome? Of course, he agreed. I can't believe they did that," she burst out emotionally, her eyes glistening with tears. She was so touched by the kind act. "You hardly *ever* see families praying together in restaurants anymore." She was choked up, yet trying to compose herself as her voice became small.

"Wow. That *is* really neat, Mom. You know, some people *do* still care about others, even in today's world. I know it's hard to believe. But, man, I'm glad they offered! We can use all the prayers we can get. And I do believe God will answer our prayers about this. He's answered everything else so far. God can do anything, you know," I encouraged her. "You just have to be patient and believe. God answers when the time is right."

We were still talking about the family at *Jimmy's Egg* when we heard the front door open.

"Hey, where you guys at?" we heard Tommy call out excitedly as he walked rapidly down the hall toward the master bedroom. Mom was resting on my bed, and I sat next to her, chatting and watching the evening world news at 5:30 p.m. He walked into the room, face lit up like a firefly. "You guys won't believe who *just called* me!" he blurted out quickly. "It was the detective, and he asked me if I was sitting down. Then he said the guy who killed Jenny just turned himself in to the Norman Police Department!" Tommy paced back and forth like a tiger in a cage. His breathing was rapid and his face was red, the excitement obviously overtaking him.

"What?! Are you kidding? Today?" we both yelled out in disbelief.

"Yep, the cops said he came into the station just a little while ago and told them he is the one who killed Jennifer!" he said, looking down at the cell phone in his hand, with a grin. "Man, they *got* him!" he exclaimed.

"How do they know he's really the killer?" I asked, suspiciously. I knew sometimes attention seekers would try to take credit for committing crimes they didn't actually commit, though just why they'd want the attention to implicate themselves was beyond me.

"Well, the Norman police said he knew things about the place where she was burned only the killer would know. So he sounds like the one," he said with a laugh.

"Oh my gosh! Thank you, God!" Mom and I both yelled out, over and over, jumping up and down like little kids. We absolutely couldn't believe what we were hearing.

"Oh, man, no way! I can't believe it happened just like that! It seems too easy!" I said, disbelieving. "And he gave details about the burn location?"

"That's what he said," Tommy answered. "He told me the guy even described some of the brush and bushes in that location. It sounds like he *is* the killer."

"Wow, this is incredible! How many people just walk into a police station and turn themselves in for murder?" I questioned. "I just cannot believe this is happening."

"Yeah, I know! I just got off the phone with the detective before I walked in the door. He said the guy told the cops he had something he had to get off his chest. He said she won't leave him alone, and he's hoping that maybe now he can have some peace," Tommy answered. "I hope it's true." He was beaming with joy; absolutely the happiest I'd ever seen him.

"All right! We have to call everybody and let them know the good news!" Mom loudly announced. Laughing, we walked into the living room and Mom began searching for her purse and phone. She was obviously thrilled and couldn't wait to start calling the rest of the family.

"Yep! We do…oh, man! You know what I just realized?" Tommy asked suddenly, with a shocked look on his face. "Those people at *Jimmy's Egg* prayed the prayer this morning for Jenny's killer to be caught. Wow! Can you believe that?" he asked softly and slowly. "And then he turns himself in, the very same day! Man, that's unbelievable!" We stood there, still and quiet for a moment, the three of us, not believing the timeline of events. We were in awe of all that had taken place. How could we not be? It was apparent; God just answered a huge prayer and in an unmistakable way.

Let's see, that makes…what, the fourth? I thought to myself. Yep, as I calculated it, I was correct. And it would be the answer to, hopefully, bring justice to Jennifer.

The excitement was overwhelming! We called everyone and told them the great news. Jenny's killer was in jail, and it was *so* incredible God chose to answer our prayer at the moment he did. It was perfect. But why should I be surprised? After all, God is a loving God who proves over and over he is with us. I couldn't help thinking of all the other answered prayers.

We were relieved the confessor was arrested but were skeptical of the things we heard. After all, there was his account of what happened and…oh, right, there was *only* his account of what happened the day he killed her. Jennifer isn't here to tell us her side, thanks to him. We realized since he turned himself in, the police would probably accept the story he gave them. After all, who was there to dispute it? According to his statement, there were supposedly no witnesses. And while he claimed he killed her and disposed of her body by himself, we'll never know if that's the truth, the whole truth, and nothing but the truth. We had doubts. Still, just having someone admit they killed her was a huge relief and wasn't something we took for granted.

Jennifer's killer, Ronald, was charged and booked; his life as he'd known it forever finished. Several years older than Jenny, we wondered if he'd kidnapped her or if he was someone she'd recently met. After all, she'd been missing for many days before the date he said he actually killed her. For all we knew, he could have held her somewhere, refusing to let her go before killing her. Whatever the details, he'd killed her and confessed. There was, at least, a decent chance for some justice now. We had something to look forward to.

THE LOVELY SOUND OF HER VOICE

As I brought a few boxes of Victorian Christmas decorations down from the attic and put them near the fireplace, I asked Mom if Jennifer ever mentioned the killer's name to her.

"No, I've never heard of him," she said. "But I knew she was seeing somebody else, someone she was dating. His name wasn't Ronald though. She never mentioned him at all. If she'd known him, she would've said something about him, wouldn't she?"

"Yeah, probably. It's interesting this Ronald guy says he knew her, but she never mentioned him to us," I agreed. "It's too bad she's not here to tell us her side of the story regarding her murder. From what I read in his statement to the police, he's trying to shift the blame away from himself, yet he is the one who has a burglary conviction in Texas and actually turned himself in on a completely different charge at the time he confessed to killing Jenny. Remember? The newspapers said he went to the police station to turn himself in on assault charges and then told the police he wanted to confess to killing her while he was there. Kind of like an afterthought. So yeah, it sounds like he's just a really great person!" I said caustically. I believed God was the reason he confessed. He had to be. After all, how many people murder someone and then turn themselves in? You don't hear that sort of thing every day.

I hurriedly reminded myself we had an evening ceremony to attend and stopped decorating. It was time to clean up and get ready. How uncanny the tree-lighting event was scheduled for the evening after Ronald turned himself in. Our attendance and observance of the event would be even more poignant. We could honor the crime victims while also telling others we finally had a break in our case! We had so much to be thankful for and couldn't wait to share the news with them! Plus, we really wanted Jennifer's ornament put on one of the remembrance trees where it belonged. I could already visualize her angel ornament dangling from a branch, slowly swaying with each movement of the tree as people bumped or moved it. Accented with silver, I loved the glitter sparkle of the white angel who held her hands together in worshipful praise of God. And I imagined Jenny's smile, if she only knew we were hanging one for her.

Hours later, Mom and I pulled into the parking lot near the entrance to the building, and Tommy arrived at nearly the same moment in his rental car. We made it. We weren't late! I nervously scanned the parking lot; I knew the butterflies I felt in my stomach were a result of being in an unfamiliar location and wondered if many from the homicide support group would be there. I deeply hoped so. I hated attending functions where I didn't know anyone and I felt a little withdrawn, a little wary of being around a bunch of strangers.

Hmmm, nobody I recognize yet, I thought as I walked toward the door leading into the facility.

Hesitantly, Mom and I walked through the doorway, looking left then right, trying to locate the room that was reserved for the event we so anxiously anticipated. Warm air enveloped us, beckoning us to walk onward, and we gratefully shook off the evening chill. The room was nearly empty, with just a few people entering ahead of us.

"Wow! This is a nice place!" Tommy excitedly remarked as he walked in behind us. "And it looks like the trees are set up over—whoa! Man, look at how many trees they have here!" he blurted out. "Geez…that's sad!"

Following his gaze, I noticed several trees already adorned with a multitude of Christmas ornaments, twinkling under the soft glow of overhead lighting fixtures. These were the ornaments with the names of crime victims. Some had actual pictures of murder victims on them, birthdates, and death dates, all commemorating someone who'd been killed at the hands of another. A lump the size of a baseball formed in my throat, and I felt the familiar ache in my heart as I tried to swallow.

"Oh, how awful!" the voice inside me cried out. "I cannot believe all of these people were killed." Sadly, I would find out later there were over 1,200 ornaments on those trees.

As I stood looking at the names and faces on the ornaments, I realized some were actual pictures of babies or small children. And I noticed several attendees, like us, placed a simple angel ornament on a tree. I couldn't believe the variety, the colors, sizes, and shapes of ornaments displayed. And I didn't know how *anyone* could easily locate their loved one's ornament again after placing it on a tree and walking away. There were just too many. My heart ached for the families represented on the trees, and I wondered how any society could heal from the overwhelming number of murders in one state. Sadly, the realization hit me. What I saw represented only a percentage of the murders committed because many people simply don't attend the yearly ceremony and put an ornament on a tree. What a sobering visual display of evil humanity. I wondered to myself how any of us sleep at night knowing somewhere in this state a person is murdered nearly every day.

Looking across the large room, I noticed a "welcome" table toward the west end. A variety of colorful cookies adorned the table, neatly arranged near paper cups and bottled water. And several event tee-shirts were folded and stacked in an orderly fashion, just waiting for interested crime-victim families to claim. I took three of the shirts since I knew all three of us would want one and then headed back toward the trees. Choosing the tree closest to the podium, we picked a spot we liked and hung Jenny's angel so she'd be slightly nestled within the branches. Then we all stood silently looking at the ornaments. I felt like an intruder, staring at the sad but beautiful reminders of the other victims represented on the trees but knew we all shared the same sorrow. We were all victims of a life altering crime.

A softly lit area toward the north wall caught my eye, and I walked over to it. Several brightly decorated poster boards lined the wall, each with murder victims' smiling faces on them. Other people noticed too and were reading what appeared in the short biographies describing the victims and their murder. And each poster showed a sad, heartbreaking story.

"Oh how horrible!" one woman blurted out, loudly. "Someone killed this young lady and these two little children!" she went on further, talking to her companion.

"Isn't that awful?" her friend agreed, sounding completely in shock.

"I don't know how *anyone* can kill someone, let alone little kids," the first one continued.

One after another, I heard people express their shock and sadness regarding the people and situations shown on the poster boards. Several tried hiding their emotions, sniffling into tissues, and walking away from the posters to look at the ornaments instead. Others stood staring at the posters with tears silently flowing down their faces as they struggled to focus on the words and pictures.

The ceremony began on schedule and what followed was a night to remember! Several people spoke, each expressing their support for violent crime victims and offering condolences to the families attending. Music filled the air, and songs to comfort the heart were sung by guest musicians, the notes lifting my spirit for those few fleeting moments. I never realized before this evening there was an extremely large group within our community who grieved the way our family was grieving, who wondered how life could ever go on and be "normal" again, the same way *we* wondered. The act of simply attending and being part of the group was healing in itself. But I also knew our lives were changed forever, and there'd be a "new normal" for us to discover for our lives. But it would be down the road. The soft melody of the last song came to a halt, and I wondered how many families attending felt the comfort of our Lord who cares for them and their murdered loved one. I could only hope and pray they *all* did.

As the ceremony concluded, I looked around once more behind the row I sat in and saw a few of the members who attended the homicide support group meeting I'd attended last month. They sat a few rows back and smiled encouragingly as their eyes met mine. But I couldn't help noticing their eyes had a certain emptiness that was undeniable. I recognized it right away. I'd seen the same emptiness in my own family's eyes, the inability to accept their loved one is gone from this life forever.

I smiled back, pretending not to notice their shiny gleam of unshed tears threatening to fall at any moment. I knew from the homicide support group meeting many of them believed God hears their prayers, but so many more could be comforted if they only *knew* it's true. I wished at that moment I could convince them our Lord hears their cries and knows their pain. I couldn't imagine *not* having his love and assurance in my soul, and I silently thanked him for being there for me. I kept remembering the words of Jesus, "Blessed are those who mourn for they shall be comforted" Matthew 5:4 (NIV).

With the passing of the remembrance ceremony, life slipped back into our somewhat normal routine, and Christmas quickly approached. After hurriedly shopping for his granddaughters' Christmas gifts, Tommy once again departed for California with the knowledge he'd be back at some point for the prosecution of Jenny's killer. His week in Oklahoma was over, but he was happy. We all were! We felt a huge relief, believing there'd be some justice down the road with a near-certain conviction.

Tommy made it out of the state just ahead of a major winter storm, with icy road conditions and snow making road travel difficult for several days. As a result, he missed Jennifer's one-year murder anniversary the following week, but the thrill of having her murder solved more than made up for the disappointment we all felt.

Back at work, I soon learned Jennifer's daughters were being remembered with Christmas gifts from some of the awesome people both within and outside our department. I truly wasn't surprised though, having the privilege of working with an amazingly generous and loving group of people. I was excited for Jennifer's little ones, knowing they'd have a Christmas they'd long remember. And the gifts were incredible! Matching bedside lamps and other bedroom décor were among the gifts wrapped with brightly colored ribbon. There were lots of toys and new clothes any child would be *thrilled* to receive on Christmas morning. And the surprise on their faces when they tore into the presents was obvious, especially when they saw even new miniature clothing wrapped up for their favorite stuffed animals. They giggled and laughed every so often, beaming from head to toe with sheer happiness. It was clear to them that many people cared about them. And the joy they experienced was a gift our family knew we could never repay.

Throughout the Christmas season, our family dealt with the loss of Jennifer as best we could. The ever-present thought "she was gone" seemed a giant hurdle to surpass, a mountain I hated remembering every morning when I woke up, knowing I had to handle the challenge again.

The house was filled with pictures of her at various ages of her life. And the fireplace hearth was no less than a shrine to Jennifer, which I set up. It was something to help me "feel better" when I looked at it. Pictures lined up in front of the fireplace soothed me and made me feel she was still with us. Sometimes they worked, sometimes they didn't. I vacillated back and forth between telling myself her pictures helped and knowing talking to God about it helped. They both did. I was beginning to learn God was really the reason I was slowly feeling better. After all, he's the one responsible for getting me through this horrible ordeal. He'd answered all my prayers, and I knew he was always with me…not Jennifer. She'll always be in my heart but can't physically be with us anymore. I understood she'd moved on to be with him. He created her, this person I love and miss. It made sense to me that since he is the source of the love I felt; I should be comforted in knowing he is always here, with me. After all, Jennifer is only a tiny *fraction* of God's love he allowed us to have for a short time. God is always with me though, no matter what. Wow, how easy this is to forget! As I trained myself to daily remember this truth, I felt so much better. I know I'll see her again through God's grace. I've never doubted it. However, it didn't stop the simple missing of her, day in and day out, or the longing to hear her voice. In fact, I caught myself searching for anything with her recorded voice on it just so I'd never forget what she sounded like. I just couldn't see a future with my not hearing her voice again! Apparently, God knew this also.

The new year arrived, and I looked forward to 2007 with renewed optimism. Not only did we have our case waiting in the court system for a probable conviction, we also had a great support group in the event we needed to bond with others in our position. To my surprise, however,

I seemed to be the only family member in Oklahoma wanting to meet with the group. I told myself it didn't matter as long as each of us dealt with our grief in a positive way. And my mom was the person I was most concerned about at the moment. Thankfully, she'd been able to reconnect with the business of daily living though helping with Katie and Emma and keeping herself busy. She was slowly returning to her former self.

It was during January, a bitter cold, windy day, when I needed Mom to drive me to work because my car fizzled out on me and had to be repaired. How I hated being without my own car! As it turned out though, Mom was available and offered to drive me to my job and pick me up at the end of the day. I watched as her car pulled up close to the door near my office, and I hopped in when she stopped the car.

"Hi, Mom. Thanks for picking me up. How was your—" I started.

"Hey…you *have* to hear this!" she interrupted abruptly, shoving a cassette tape into the car's cassette player and twisting the volume knob. She drove away from the hospital, glancing back and forth between the road and the cassette player. Along with some rather annoying background noise, I heard someone talking. It sounded like me.

"Listen!" she ordered excitedly. "Who does that sound like? I found this today in a box I had packed away," she rushed on.

Listening for a few seconds, I guessed, "Me? It sounds like a tape I made years ago. That's me," I answered.

"No," she responded, "it's Jennifer."

"Mom, it's me. It sounds just like me," I argued.

I concentrated, turning the volume up even more and leaned closer to a speaker. That's when I recognized her voice. I couldn't believe it, but it was Jennifer! I'd prayed so hard for some kind of keepsake recording with her voice on it, and here it was. And the strange part was… she sounded just like me. I couldn't believe it; I'd never noticed it before. I listened for a few moments before turning it off. It wasn't a good copy because of all the background noise, but it was *something*.

"I'm going to listen to it again when we get to the house, Mom," I told her while straining to catch every word. I was stunned! "We should get some copies of this made on CDs too. I'm sure the whole family will want a copy."

Astounded at what she'd found, Mom explained she'd found it in a box tucked away in a closet. She couldn't believe Jennifer recorded it and didn't tell her about it. Evidently, she'd recorded it a few years earlier while she was home alone on Mother's Day of 2004. Covering several topics, she chatted along on the tape, chronicling her day while doing laundry and cooking. Along with her comments about her small daughters' most recent accomplishments in "toddler world" and her observation of the lovely yet unpredictable Oklahoma weather, she made an unusual statement, "I don't know who I'm making this tape for *[pause]* maybe you." I couldn't believe it! How incredible! I'd nearly torn my house apart looking for my old answering machine, and suddenly, a tape is discovered in a box—a tape with Jennifer talking to no one in particular for approximately thirty minutes. She talked about making dinner for Mom and how Mom deserved to have a great Mother's Day. To my own embarrassment, she even mentioned the movie she'd checked out for Katie, one I borrowed and still had at my house. I remember her leaving messages for me, saying, "I need that movie back. Call me please!" But the most astounding part of the tape came toward the end. She mentioned something she'd discussed with Mom the previous week regarding a program my mom had seen on TV. It left an obvious impression on Jenny. It stated that some catastrophic event was predicted by someone to take place on Earth in the year 2012. Jenny had obviously been thinking about the prediction and said, *"I don't know if that's really gonna happen. All I know is if I'm still here then I want to be right with God."* I couldn't understand her saying this at her tender age. Where did she think she could be if not here? However, it comforted me hearing it, as I realized, she really knew God and wanted a closer relationship with him. I just needed to keep reminding my mother she *is* with God now, and incredibly happy.

Arriving back at the house, I raced to put the tape in and listened again. She sounded great! And it didn't even matter what she said. I was just deliriously happy to be hearing *something* from her—*anything!* I sat listening with a grateful heart, reminding myself God had answered yet another prayer. Incredibly, he just kept the blessings coming. Let's see…this was…the fifth one. I didn't understand how I could be so blessed. I certainly didn't deserve it. He not only listened, he also kept answering our prayers. I made a silent promise to thank him each time I realized an answer to a prayer. And that seemed to be happening often.

For weeks I drove back and forth to work listening to the CD we had copied from the tape Jenny recorded.

Just listening to her voice made me feel like she was still here, near her family. But there was just one problem with listening to the whole recording. At *some* point, it came to an end. And then I'd just start it over…*again*. Finally, after several weeks of listening to it daily and having much of it memorized, I realized I needed to put it away for a time and try to refocus on the living. After all, spring was approaching—glorious, earth-warming spring! And *this* spring, Katie turned five, with the vocabulary of a ten-year-old and an attitude to match. She constantly amazed me, such distinguished conversation from a "small fry." She wanted to know how everything worked, what everything was, where everything came from, and everything else in between. She was a junior master at *Twenty Questions*!

"What's this, Aunt KayKay?" she quizzed me while squatting down, gazing at something small on the ground one warm afternoon. The tiny cracked acorn shell lay partially hidden between a few old brown leaves near a tree. It was barely visible, but she quickly caught sight of it as she scanned the ground for anything unknown to her.

"Oh, that? That's just an old acorn shell. It used to have an acorn in it. It's like a nut. You know…those things squirrels eat during the winter," I replied. I sat nearby, watching her.

Staring at it intently, she softly answered in her best attempt at sounding melancholy. "I used to have a squirrel," she stated in a flat tone. "But then he died…cuz I didn't feed him any nuts." I burst out laughing, shocked at what she said. She looked so *serious* when she said it.

"Listen here, silly! You never had a squirrel, and I can't believe you're trying to make me think you did." I tried to sound stern, but ended up laughing instead.

"I didn't?" she asked.

"No. You didn't," I answered.

"Oh...well...I *thought* I did!" she defended herself, laughing boldly at the obvious mistake she'd made. Tousle-haired and twinkly eyed, she reminded me of her mom, who had the same inquisitive nature when she was little. Katie glowed with enthusiasm when she asked questions, trying to learn everything in one day. I remembered similarly funny moments like this one with Jennifer. One memory in particular stood out. Jennifer was about six or seven years old when she walked out of my bedroom with a pair of my high-heeled shoes on and an old ball cap perched crookedly on her head. What a hoot she was, trying to walk into the living room without stumbling. And just before falling, her shrill voice squeaked out, "Oops!"

She could never be replaced, but I knew as I looked into the inquisitive brown eyes of her small daughter, we were blessed to still have a little bit of Jennifer with us.

WHAT IS THIRD-DEGREE ARSON?

Anxiously, our family waited for word from the district attorney's office about a preliminary hearing for the defendant. We learned it's a very common thing for postponements within the judicial system. We found out it wouldn't be until July. During those months of waiting for the hearing, we kept wondering just how it would all turn out. Would he just admit he'd killed her and then go straight to prison? Would he get the death penalty? After all, he'd killed her very violently; it would only be right if he did! The waiting was extremely difficult and the months dragged by. We couldn't wait to see her killer in court…to see with our own eyes the kind of person who viciously attacks an unarmed young woman and destroys her body as he'd done to Jennifer.

July 10, 2007, proved a huge eye opener as to what happens during preliminary hearings. We'd already been told that the victim's family could not stare at the defendant, make any noises, chew gum, cry, or show any kind of emotion. And yet it seemed amazingly unfair the defendant could look around the room while talking to his attorney during the proceedings. It just didn't seem quite right to our family. I couldn't believe he was allowed to show emotion either. Sitting with his Bible on the table close to him, it was obvious to me he was playing the part of a repentant "nice guy" with a sad expression while wearing wrist and ankle shackles. How relieved I was Tommy was able to come back for the hearing, to observe the court proceedings.

Witnesses for the state were heard, their stories overwhelmingly confirming his guilt. One after another, the details of his confession were shared with the court. Some of them were shocking: the attack on her small body (she weighed somewhere between 100 and 120 pounds) and the mere fact he could do what he'd done to her with a knife and his own two hands! It was brutal just hearing it. How could any person stab someone, cut them, and then burn their body? What kind of human was he? Most murders we'd heard of in the news were gunshot killings, which were horrific enough. But what kind of person takes pleasure in using their hands in actually feeling the life flow out of someone? We knew we were in the same room with a monster…pure evil. There could be no other way to look at it. And yet he turned himself in! God definitely had a hand in this happening, a *big* hand in it.

A huge disappointing reminder came at the moment the charges were read, however. We were told ahead of time what he'd be charged with, but it was still hard to accept. To charge him with her murder was obvious, but it also seemed to our family he should be held accountable for the horrific things he'd done to her body.

"One count *first-degree murder*, one count *third-degree arson*, and one count *removal of a human body*," stated the judge.

Unbelievably, those were the only crimes he could be charged with. And the charge of third-degree arson was only because he'd burned property worth more than $50, the field her body was lying on when he set her on fire. There was no mention he'd burned her body. As frustrating as it was for our family, the district attorney's office wasn't happy about it either. Their hands were tied. They understood our pain over her body's desecration and reassured us the killer would have been charged with that crime had it been against the law in Oklahoma. Thank heavens the DA's office was able to charge him with removing her body from the location where she was killed and taking her to a different place, the place where he burned her. It was the best they could do, plus charging him with the third-degree arson (which only applies to *property*).

Another thing our courts fail to consider is the emotional damage to the families. It really made us feel like they saw the property as being more valuable than Jenny's body. What other message from a third-degree arson charge could we receive? We realized the killer was charged with her murder, but it just didn't seem a strong enough charge considering he'd tried to destroy her identity too. It was obvious he didn't care she had a family who'd be crushed by his unconscionable actions. He'd made sure we couldn't have an open-casket viewing to say good-bye the way most people do. We buried a casket with desecrated remains in it, only a few bones. So…no traditional closure for our family.

After the judge agreed there was plenty of reason to proceed with a trial, based on the evidence given during the preliminary hearing, the hearing was adjourned. I couldn't wait to get out of the courtroom so our family could discuss what we'd heard. As we stood to exit the room, I glanced over at the defendant and saw and heard an exchange I couldn't believe! One of the police officers, who'd given his statement about what Ron told him during his confession in Norman, walked over toward Ron and asked him how he was doing. Then he said something to the effect of, "You're looking better than when I saw you last." Small talk! They were making small talk, right there in the courtroom in front of the victim's family. Yet we were not allowed to say a word in court or "stare" at the defendant or cry, chew gum, etc. How unfair it seemed…and how disappointing to realize some of what I'd heard about the judicial system was really true. It did appear the criminals have more rights than the victims. Apparently, the defendants have the right to talk in the courtroom and visit with the witnesses. That really bothered us.

Were we worked up! Our family talked nonstop about the fact Jenny's burned body was not mentioned in court. We couldn't believe the judge on the case kept referring to the "property" as being burned and talked about the value of the "property." It just seemed to our family Jenny's burned body was overlooked in that regard. Yet we knew the district attorney's office charged the killer with everything in their power. After all, they don't create the laws. They assist with criminal investigations and prosecute charges when laws are broken. We did appreciate all the information they gave us, however, explaining everything we had questions about, through each step of the process.

"Oklahoma *really* needs a law to make it a crime to do what he did to Jenny's body, you know it?" Tommy blurted out in frustration for the hundredth time as we walked back to the car from the court. We knew ahead of time what to expect in the courtroom, but it was so painful hearing he couldn't and therefore wouldn't be held responsible for burning her body.

"I know. Somebody needs to push for a new law. It's so painful families have to see the court system overlook that kind of crime," I agreed. I could only imagine how difficult the rest of the court process was going to be. I dreaded it. Yet I wanted it over and done. I just wanted him found guilty and executed. In fact, the way I saw it, the vicious attack should qualify him for the death penalty since she probably suffered so much while dying. At least I hoped it would. I couldn't *wait* for sentencing day and frequently fantasized about him pleading with the judge for his life. I wanted him to lose what he'd taken from Jennifer…a life. And I believed God would bring justice.

Strangely, I was torn spiritually regarding his confession. I knew I had to forgive him for the pain he caused me by murdering my sister, but I didn't want to. Then just when I thought I'd never be able to, it finally happened. It was hard…*extremely* hard! But how else could I expect God to forgive all the sin I'd committed in my lifetime, all the trespassing I'd done, if I wouldn't forgive Ron? I couldn't speak for anyone else in my family, but I knew it was what God wanted from all of us, from everyone on earth. Plus the forgiveness wasn't for Ron's benefit anyway, it was for mine. It would help me move forward with *some* semblance of peace and help me heal.

I realized, however, forgiving someone and desiring their payment to society were two different things. The fact he'd confessed didn't change anything regarding his earthly punishment. He still had to be held accountable for what he'd done. Plus there was the fact he'd face God in the afterlife when he'd be judged along with everyone else. It would end there. In the meantime, he wasn't off the hook. He had a debt to pay for killing Jennifer, and I was glad he'd have to pay it. I just didn't know how I could wait for that day to arrive!

TEXAS HAS IT, SO WHY CAN'T WE?

The sizzling hot month of August once again beat down upon Oklahoma, and as I drove to Jenny's grave after work, I thought of a joke I heard regarding days like this, not long ago:

You know how hot it is? It's so hot that a hound dog was chasin' a rabbit, and they were both walkin'! I laughed out loud to myself, thinking it was amazing I found *anything* funny about hundred-degree temperatures. However, despite the heat, I wanted to go to Jennifer's grave to be "still" with her memory for a few moments. After all, it had been a whole year since we'd buried her already. How quickly the year passed! So much had happened since we laid her to rest, but there was still so much to finish. Her case was still open; the courts were waiting for lab results to confirm whether it was Jenny's blood evidence they'd found at Ron's home at the time of her murder. Still, I didn't mind waiting awhile if it meant the prosecution could prove it was her blood. In the event Ron pushed for a trial, I knew it would still have to be proven he killed her. And his confession didn't mean he wasn't going to try to get the best deal possible.

"Hey, Jenny," I said softly as I approached her grave marker. Nothing but silence and an occasional chirp of a bird answered. I stood, staring at the marker, memorizing the gold lettering stating her name, date of birth, and death. A small gold angel with a trumpet stood out boldly near Jennifer's name. What a great place to come to, to think about her…and talk to God.

I wondered how and *if* it could even be possible to get some kind of law in Oklahoma to make it a crime for someone to cut or burn a body after they'd killed them. I believed it *must* be possible. After all, one of the women in our support group had a law passed recently so family members could wear a button in court with their loved one's picture on it. That was a major accomplishment, considering before this new law, only the defendant (and not his murder victim) could be seen in court, looking clean and polished (although wearing the jail jumpsuit, of course). In the past, case after case, the murder victims remained faceless (unless viewed in a crime scene photo)…a heartbreaking sorrow to victims' families.

I paced, circling Jenny's grave. I really wanted to pursue a new law. But how could I do that? Should I write a letter to my legislators? Call them, perhaps?

Focusing on Jennifer's grave, I finally bent down and placed the plastic dark red cherry blossom arrangement into her brass vase. The miniature oval-shaped ceramic picture of her the monument company had attached to her marker seemed to smile back at me. I reluctantly said good-bye, gently touching her picture with my fingers. I couldn't get the thought of a new law out of my mind and drove home thinking, if God thought this was important, then it would become a new law in Oklahoma. It was that simple.

Over the next few weeks, the Oklahoma winds blew in a new season, and the weather began changing. Although I love the fall scenery, my allergies flared up in a nasty way. The sore throat, sneezing, watery eyes, and head congestion all led to one place…the doctor's office. I felt miserable and knew, despite the several prescriptions to relieve the symptoms, I'd be out of commission for a few days. Unfortunately, the symptoms hung on for weeks, and I realized I'd have to miss my very first *national day of remembrance for murder victims,* which was scheduled for September 25, 2007. I sat at home the evening of the event, coughing, blowing my nose, and sniffling, all the while wishing I could attend.

"Hey, you missed a really good service this evening, Mary," my friend Lena contacted me on my cell phone after the remembrance ended. She was a high-energy lady, a friend I'd recently met from both my church and the homicide support group. Although she'd lost her own dad at the hands of a drunk driver, she maintained a cheerful spirit, lifting others up who were in a similar situation. Her enthusiasm bubbled over as she mentioned a senator was the keynote speaker during the event. She was thrilled because he'd spoken with some of the homicide victim families afterwards.

"We had a chance to tell him about some of the issues we think need to be added as new Oklahoma laws." She chatted on rapidly, stating the group mentioned the lack of a law against desecrating a dead body. "He actually listened and seemed interested! He couldn't believe what happened to Jennifer isn't a crime." Lena was clearly impressed he took such a keen interest in crime victims and her enthusiasm increased, along with the pitch of her voice. "He said you can contact him or, at least, find out who your senator and representatives are and try to contact them. Someone will listen," she urged.

"Okay, I will. Good idea," I laughed. I thought she'd slow down, but her excitement was not to be contained. "I'll give it a try, but you know, sometimes people seem like they're interested in making changes when they really aren't," I pointed out. I didn't want to sound pessimistic, but I knew it was all up to God as far as the timing and whether or not it would happen. And I didn't want to be disappointed if things didn't move as quickly as I'd have liked. Still, I couldn't wait to find out exactly who I needed to contact.

My mind raced as I phoned Tommy to let him know about the interest of the senator who attended the murder remembrance. He was thrilled, impatient to get in touch with someone *himself*. He desperately wanted to get a law passed and wanted to get started as soon as possible. None of us wanted another family going through what we'd gone through at the preliminary hearing, the obvious fact of her burned, desecrated body with no law to address or punish for it.

"I'm going to start contacting some people, maybe e-mail them and see if they're interested. There has to be *someone* in the Oklahoma legislature who'll see the importance of this kind of law," he pointed out. "And I'll contact the senator you told me about. We should be able to find his office listed on the Internet and get his e-mail address. We both need to get on that quickly and see if there's any way it can be done during this year's session." I could almost hear the wheels of his mind turning as his suggestions flowed toward me over the air waves.

"Sounds great!" I agreed. "Let me know what you find out, and I'll do some checking too."

We were excited, wanting to do something we knew would help other families in our position. But uppermost in my mind was the upcoming arraignment, scheduled for October 9, 2007. As it turned out, our court date ended up being another preliminary hearing, when the blood evidence results would be presented to the court. Although those results didn't prove it was Jenny's blood, they *did* reveal the devious mind of her killer. He'd apparently cleaned up the blood with some kind of solution, which made it impossible to even tell it was human. What a disappointment! Nonetheless, we found out then his case was scheduled for a pretrial conference in November. That meant the trial couldn't be too far down the road.

In the meantime, I searched the website for Oklahoma State senators and sent out a few e-mails. I also made a point of sending one to Senator Jim Reynolds, the person I'd been told who attended the service the month before. It was October 15 already, and I worried I might have waited too long. After all, I knew there was a deadline regarding the proposal of new legislation. And Tommy had sent an e-mail to Senator Reynolds days before I did. I hoped I wasn't too late.

Despite the fact I'd had no response from the other legislators, only days later, I was delightfully surprised when I received a brief message from Senator Reynolds stating he'd get back in touch with me. He'd read my e-mail! I was ecstatic! I could already imagine having the law in place and law officials charging guilty, hardened criminals with it. We just had to be patient and see what our new ally, the senator, was able to accomplish.

I found myself on the computer often, searching for cases resembling Jennifer's, cases involving desecration of the deceased. Maybe, just maybe, there was another state with a similar law. I searched...and finally...*jackpot!* I found it. Texas had one brand-new law less than a year old! Theirs was called, *"the Jennifer Cave act."* And ironically, the *Texas* Jennifer was nearly my sister's age and had been brutally dismembered after being murdered. I felt a wave of nausea imagining her family's pain. I read on, noticing it went into effect on September 1, 2007, so it was extremely new. If only we could convince Oklahoma to pass a similar law! I wondered if forwarding the news article on to the senator would help convince him and his colleagues this was a good thing for Oklahoma to have too. I made the quick decision to send it to him along with a note asking him to read it, asking him why Oklahoma didn't deserve to have a law like this. I prepared the e-mail, hesitating only a moment before hitting the Send button. Then I exhaled! I was nervous, not wanting to seem pushy or demanding. In fact, I didn't realize I'd been holding my breath until I pushed the button. The way I saw it, the only thing left to do now was pray for it to pass through the system, to be accepted by all who were involved in creating and passing new legislation. And we certainly did pray!

"God, please let there be a new law in Oklahoma, one telling criminals they face additional punishment if they treat humans as garbage, something to be burned, cut, or thrown away. Please give the lawmakers in our state open eyes to see anything less treats murder victims as though they have no worth, no identity. They are someone's daughter, sister, or mother or someone's son, brother, or father."

I thought of the professional forensic artists who work with the mutilated bodies of the dead, carefully cleaning away burned or decomposed flesh in order to reconstruct a face and a head. How sad those people have to see, firsthand, the evil treatment these human bodies suffer. They touch them, clean them, and hold them, knowing they are the last to lovingly care for the broken bodies of someone else's loved one. They also know when they came into this world they were most likely deeply loved. What an awful ending to a beautiful beginning, and what a heart-wrenching task for a forensic artist.

Little Jennifer drinking Mom's tea

With Grandpa Tommy Collins

Summer pool time fun

Skiing with Daddy and Grandma

At Grandma's house

Jennifer as a teenager

A DAY OF RECKONING

The pretrial conference was set for November 14, 2007, and I hoped our family would be allowed to attend, if for no other reason than to see if Ron might squirm (this time) in the courtroom. I didn't believe he'd be *too* uncomfortable though, after seeing him at the preliminary hearing. He had appeared to be pretty calm and relaxed. I also wanted to see him sentenced to the death penalty. I was anxious for it. I fell asleep at night praying I'd hear the judge say, "You are hereby sentenced to death…" It seemed only fair to me. However, a small sadistic part of me also thought life in prison without parole would be a good thing too. I even occasionally fantasized about him eating only bread and drinking water to sustain him until he died. Or better yet, I'd *really* get happy thinking of him on a chain gang, sweating profusely with the backbreaking labor I'd seen in movies, while wearing a striped black-and-white cotton outfit! I could just imagine the contented smile that must have spread with an incredible slowness across my face, my eyes glazing over as though I were in a trance…

I prayed he'd get nothing less than life in prison so he'd have to live with the knowledge…the memories of what he'd done, for the rest of his life while incarcerated.

I wondered if he dreamed about Jennifer as I did. Did he ask her forgiveness? Did he feel remorse? If so, was it real? It felt so strange, hoping for such extreme punishment for a person and wondering (so often) if he thought of his victim. I jumped around, emotionally, one day wishing the worst for him and the next wondering if he were praying and feeling bad about what he'd done. I wondered if he thought about his life after death.

As a Christian, I knew I should see murder as one of many sins. But murder seemed so much *worse* than other sins to me. And yet I knew if he were truly remorseful and asked God's forgiveness, he would be forgiven. Equally important, he'd have to forgive others who'd sinned against him *and* accept Christ as his Savior. Whether or not he repented, he'd still get the death penalty or maybe life in prison without parole—I hoped. Either way, he'd be punished. Justice had to be served.

I felt myself practically float through the days following the senator's response to my e-mail. And a week later, I was still reveling in the possibility of a new law he might initiate when we got the surprising phone call from the district attorney's office, saying the defendant was agreeing to a plea bargain! The assistant DA handling the case contacted Tommy, my mother, and me, conducting a multi-person phone call so we could all discuss the pros and cons of accepting one. I was adamantly opposed. Tommy wasn't thrilled either. However, the bargain was for the defendant to get life in prison, *without parole*, if he pled guilty and avoided a trial.

The assistant district attorney, Mr. Ackley, explained what a plea bargain meant: "You know, if this case does go to trial, we'll have to prove he committed at least one of the aggravating factors, for capital punishment (the death penalty). And I'm not absolutely sure any of those can be proven to a jury, even the possibility of proving the murder was especially heinous or involved torture. We don't know for certain she suffered before she died, as it's described in the law, so that's not really a feasible point to try to prove."

We knew Ackley was a long-time assistant DA for Oklahoma County and could probably recite the aggravating circumstances in his sleep, along with many other rules and laws applicable to cases such as ours. So we didn't question his knowledge. We just didn't like the idea of Ron getting to *live* while Jennifer couldn't. Plus I couldn't believe Jennifer's death could not be proven as being heinous, causing her to suffer before death. After all, she'd been hit over the head several times with a bat and then stabbed vertically into the top of her head before having her throat cut. Ron had even admitted she'd struggled with him.

Despite the details of her death, I believed Gary and trusted he was the best judge of the situation. I knew he'd recommend what he thought was truly the best route to take, in any case.

"So, when will the sentencing be, assuming the prosecution goes forward with the plea deal?" I asked him.

"I don't know yet, but I'll get back in touch with you tomorrow with the date," he promised. "It will probably be very soon, maybe the end of the week."

"Wow, that *is* fast," I said. "At least we wouldn't have to go through the frustration of a trial, with it dragging out for the next two to three years, huh?"

"That's right," he agreed. "And you could put this part of your grief behind you. He'd be locked away for life."

We discussed and haggled over the pros and cons a few more minutes and then agreed with going along the route of the plea bargain. It wasn't exactly what we wanted, but he wouldn't be getting a short prison sentence either. Now all we had to do was prepare for his sentencing date and write our victim impact statements. Everything was moving very quickly, and we were anxious to have it finished. We wanted to see him and hear him being sentenced. And we wanted to have *him* hear what *we* felt about losing Jennifer, a loss he was responsible for.

The excitement of the previous days was overwhelming, and the defendant's day of reckoning was quickly approaching. It was set for October 26, 2007, and before we knew it, we were walking into the Oklahoma County District Attorney's Office, waiting for Ronald's sentencing to take place. We made sure to bring tissues, victim impact statements, and our buttons with Jennifer's picture on them that we were now allowed to wear inside the courtroom. We were meeting with a few of the assistant DA's prior to sentencing, in the "family room." It almost seemed too good to be true! It would all be over soon, only a matter of another hour or so.

Jennifer, I wish somehow you knew what's happening here today. He's going to admit what he did to you, in court, and be sentenced for it, I thought to myself, wishing she could hear me. I felt a lump swell in my throat just thinking of her. I fought back the tears and glanced at my mother. Poor Mom. How many times since we'd buried Jennifer had I heard or seen her crying, wanting her daughter back? And all she had to look forward to for Jennifer was this final day. We'd *all* waited since the day we buried her…for her murderer's sentencing day. It wasn't heartwarming, and it wasn't a reunion with Jennifer, but it *was something*. It was payment of a sort, for what he'd taken from us…and for Jennifer. She deserved this payment, and we needed it. And hopefully, it would bring us nearer to closure.

The brief meeting with Ackley before sentencing was reassuring. Along with Assistant District Attorney Scott Rowland, they explained what would happen in court, where we'd sit, and asked if we had any questions. Then they reminded us Ron's family would possibly be in the courtroom, and we were *not* required to speak with them. They'd be sitting in the section closest to the defendant, and our family would be near the door exiting the room.

"How will we know when we're supposed to read our impact statements?" Mom asked, looking tired and gaunt. She had dark circles under her eyes, and I could tell she hadn't slept much the night before. She looked worn out already.

"The judge will let you know. She'll announce it when she's ready for you to go up there in front of her. So don't be nervous. She hears these all the time. You'll be okay," Ackley reassured her.

"Oh, I have a question," Tommy half raised his hand into the air to get Ackley's attention. "Will Ron get to say anything to the court or our family when we're in there?"

"The judge will call him up to the bench to formally sentence him, and at that point, she may ask him if he has anything to say to the court," Ackley replied. "But he won't be allowed to walk over toward your family or anything like that. He'll be standing in front of *her*."

"Oh, okay. That's good. Just wondering...," Tommy said as though he were searching for the right words. He hesitated a moment and then continued. "I mean... he won't try to direct any conversation toward us or talk to us, will he? I know *I* wouldn't have anything nice to say to *him*," he stated forcefully with a small laugh, his eyes gleaming. Tommy told us many times before this day exactly what he'd like to say to Ronald if he were in a room alone with him! In fact, we'd all have liked to vent our rage against him. However, we had to believe the legal system would serve the people as it was meant to, that he'd pay for his crime in prison for the remainder of his life.

"I understand your concerns, but no, that won't be happening. He's aware when he's in court he's supposed to approach the judge's bench only. So that won't be a problem," Ackley stated confidently. He looked around the room for a brief moment, searching for an indication any of us might have more questions, and then said, "Okay, let's all head into the courtroom and get this started, if no one has anything else."

Boy was I nervous! The simple act of walking into the courtroom and taking a seat was enough to make me shake. I glanced toward the defense table and saw Ron sitting in his seat, stone-faced, trying to avoid eye contact by looking toward the judge's bench. My nerves got the best of me, and I anxiously pulled apart a tissue as I tried to calm myself. Then I heard a sniffle to my left and realized Ron's family was already seated in their section of the courtroom. I was overcome by feelings of sadness for them...I couldn't imagine being in *their* shoes either.

They were all crying softly. I noticed an older couple who must have been his parents and a couple of young women I assumed were his sisters or other relatives. They looked *extremely* sad but didn't say a word. How awful for them to see their son or brother in this predicament, on his way to prison for life. I'd never even given a thought to how his family would be taking all this, wrapped up as I was in my own grief. To my relief though, they didn't look our way, and I tried to refocus my attention elsewhere.

Tommy and Mom sat on the bench in front of me in the very front row, along with other family members. I was happy to sit behind them, wanting to just disappear into the bench I sat on. I couldn't understand why I felt like I was at a public hanging. I'd never seen anyone sentenced before and didn't realize I'd feel so sad about the entire scope of the situation. *Why did he do this to us? Why did he do that to her? Why did he hurt his own family this way?*

The grief in the room felt like an enormous weight, an *anchor*, dragging me down and giving me the sensation of what drowning must feel like. I don't know how much more cracked and broken a heart can feel. And the strangest part was my unexpected feelings of compassion for his family. We weren't the only family hurting, and it was very obvious.

Thankfully, we didn't have to wait long for the proceedings to begin, but I did wonder whether or not my mom would be able to actually stand up and read her impact statement without completely losing it. We were surrounded by friends, and I thanked God for each of them. Shelba, the homicide advocate, sat near me, assuring me she'd be with us for the entire sentencing. Possessing a strong and positive outlook, she instilled a "you can get through anything" attitude in me, reminded me God never does leave us. I knew he was there, in the courtroom...still caring and loving us.

I also noticed Glenda, my friend from our homicide support group, enter the courtroom. I smiled and motioned for her to come over toward the bench I sat on. To my delight, she found a seat near me and Shelba. She smiled encouragingly, offering me a tissue, but I held up an entire box of tissues Shelba had given me earlier to show her I was covered in that area. I was thrilled to see she cared enough to be here with me, and I felt so honored to have her show up for this day. I realized I really was extremely blessed with good friends, loving family, and awesome district attorneys who were not only very polished at what they did for a living but also *cared about the families* they worked with daily.

The judge declared court in session and then addressed Ron and the attorneys. I strained to hear every word. She was going over the terms of the plea bargain, verifying he understood everything he'd agreed to do. Did he understand he was sentenced to life in prison without the possibility of parole?

"Yes, Your Honor," I heard him say, several times.

It was unnaturally quiet in the courtroom despite the occasional comments of the judge, the attorneys, and the defendant. But every so often, I heard Tommy or Mom break into a soft sob, trying to contain the pain they felt. I knew Tommy was still having a difficult struggle to come to terms with Jenny's death. He seemed changed...broken and horribly hurt one moment, and then raging the next about how he'd love to get his hands on the man who had killed his daughter. I knew he wouldn't approach or attempt an attack on Jennifer's killer though. He would "get his day in the courtroom" through his victim impact statement, the civilized way. However, I half expected him to yell at Ron, to tell him loudly what he thought of him. I watched...waiting for it, *expecting it*, but it didn't happen. He sat still, observing the process and waiting for his turn to speak.

Every few minutes, I glanced toward Ron's family and noticed they were still very emotional. I couldn't help but think they were crying for him and the fact he'd ruined his life. I imagined them missing him at the family holiday dinners and get-togethers as well as with daily routines. For all I knew, he could be their only son. I felt more tears burn my eyes and told myself to stop being such an emotional wreck. I wanted to focus.

"If there's anything you'd like to say to the court, you may do it now," the judge advised Ron. She sounded very compassionate yet firm. I'd heard many wonderful things about her and wasn't disappointed to find they were true. She *was* a kind and warm judge, very personable. It also seemed she was taking note of everything going on in the room by the way she watched the families grieving, both his and ours. He stood, slowly dragging ankle chains with him toward her bench.

I stared at him, not wanting to forget a single moment or move he made. *All* eyes were on him. I briefly wondered if everything we'd heard about his confession was true. We were told he believed Jenny haunted him at night, preventing him from sleeping, before he turned himself in. I couldn't imagine the kind of dreams he had since he killed her. The sick movie reel would undoubtedly play over and over. And having a belief God works through dreams, I could understand how he could have been haunted by what he'd done. God could make it so. He could make any dream occur. Between the awful dreams, hallucinations or whatever you want to call them, and the prayers for the capture of Jennifer's killer, God delivered! He made sure Ron turned himself in.

Pacing and looking highly anxious, Ron started talking. He wasn't exactly formidable looking. Standing at around five feet eight or nine inches, he looked normal… not like a killer at all. Except he was. But then, Jenny was short with a small frame. Next to him, she probably looked tiny. I noticed his head was shaved, and he was fairly pale. Hanging his head slightly, he began by calmly apologizing to the court for the crimes he'd committed. (Of course, I felt that apologies weren't enough. I wanted him to be unhappy, to *suffer*, as we were all suffering.)

And then I noticed…he was crying! Crying! And he *kept* crying, talking about how he'd ruined his life and how he wished he'd never done the things he'd done. He mentioned the pain he put everyone through. And he cried more, loudly! It was as if a dam burst, and he couldn't stop. I couldn't believe my ears or my eyes! He was slightly bent over at the waist, as if he'd pass out from the extreme emotion of the moment and the gut-wrenching pain of the knowledge he was going away for life.

The emotions I was reading in him were so strong and seemed very authentic. It was then, at the same time, I believed he was sorry for what he'd done. I heard his family crying more loudly now but couldn't take my eyes off Ron to look over in their direction. It was a spectacle, a shock, a remorseful and desperate man I was seeing.

Was the remorse for Ron though or was it for Jennifer? I felt the wet tears running down my face, and noticed I seemed to be the only person in my family still crying at that moment. Everyone I looked at seemed hypnotized by the display they were seeing. Ron seemed to truly want to impress on everyone present he was repentant for what he'd done. But could he be believed? I never expected sentencing day to turn out this way. I didn't expect the scene we were witnessing! And I didn't expect to feel what I did at that moment either. I actually felt bad for him. He appeared to be *suffering*...but then again, wasn't it what we'd wanted?

To my surprise though, his suffering didn't bring the satisfaction I'd anticipated. I couldn't tell if he was sorry for himself, the whole situation, or for Jennifer. In fact, *he never even mentioned her name. I just felt empty.*

COMPASSION ALL AROUND

"Please take your seat, Mr. Weston," the judge ordered. "Be seated!" she raised her voice. She was having trouble getting his attention. "That's enough! Mr. Weston!"

I couldn't believe the emotional turmoil he was obviously in. He cried and cried *loudly*, as if to make a last minute effort for some kind of leniency. He even reminded the judge he turned himself in, as if that might somehow influence her to change the sentence.

"Sit down, Mr. Weston!" she ordered, very loudly this time. Sniffling and trying to compose himself, he shuffled back to his seat. For a few moments, the courtroom was quiet. It was apparent everyone in the room was stunned at what they'd just witnessed. After all, he must've stood near the bench (pacing and stating his regrets) a minimum of ten minutes. She had to *make* him sit down! It was like he was emotionally fighting for his life, the way Jennifer fought physically for hers. I couldn't believe it! I wondered if he saw the similarity…the awful feeling of not being in control of one's own life. He was getting a taste of what she probably felt—helpless…unable to save herself.

My nerves were all over the place. I could feel the sweat forming on the palms of my hands, and I had a slight twitch above my left eye, annoying me beyond belief. I almost dreaded the next phase of sentencing and started feeling a slight queasiness come over my stomach. It was all so stressful, sad, liberating, and many other emotions all stirred together.

"Okay. I'll hear the family's impact statements now, if you'd still like to give them. You can read them here in front of the bench," the judge informed us while sliding her paperwork aside.

Just as I'd anticipated, Tommy was up first. I knew he was anxious to have his voice heard in court, to have *Ron* hear his voice in court, so I braced myself for the verbal whiplashing I was sure we'd all witness. But he was surprisingly calm…calm, and *razor sharp* in his comments regarding what he thought of Ron.

"First of all, I want to say that my *only* child was taken from me," he said. Then his voice gave way to the flood of emotion welling up inside him. He cleared his throat and continued reading his statement, struggling to get the words out clearly. "Every day, I wake up and remember I won't ever be allowed to see her again, not in this life. Her two little girls will grow up without their mother and will always want to know why their mother can't be here with them. What happened to my daughter is unimaginable and something no father should have to live through." He continued, indignantly, his voice getting louder. "I also want Ron to know that he is a *coward*, afraid to choose for *himself* what he chose for Jennifer. He chose death for my daughter and life for himself!" His hands shook with grief, and I wondered how he could continue.

I looked at both families and noticed Tommy's words caused a renewed outpour of emotion. Ron's family cried every bit as hard as our family, if not harder for a few moments, and I understood their pain. At least, I thought I did.

God bless those poor people! They've lost someone too in a sense, I prayed silently as I blew my nose. I was having a hard time focusing on what Tommy was saying because of all our crying.

I thought about the fact their family and ours were both going through a similarly hard time. This whole heartbreaking period in our lives was so much like a storm, which kept going, an extremely difficult storm to endure!

Suddenly a song I loved, called "Praise You in This Storm" (Casting Crowns) came to mind. I'd felt a strong connection to the lyrics since we buried Jennifer, and I held them close to my heart. In fact, I've never heard a song which so completely captured my feelings about Jenny's death and our family's suffering because of it. The song reminds us that God is always with us, no matter what. And I knew he *was* with us…always. I only had to think back and remember all the prayers God had answered since Jenny disappeared. To add to the blessings God delivered, Ron would be going to prison for the rest of his life. It was one more thing we'd prayed for, life in prison without parole or the death penalty, for her killer.

How thankful I was God had chosen to deliver some of his answers to me through dreams. Those answers gave me the strength to keep pushing on, always remembering he would not forget us. The answers were a great thing, leading us to Jennifer and justice for her murder. How could I ever doubt these dreams were from God? I knew the scripture in the Bible James 1:17 (NIV) "Every good and perfect gift is from above, coming down from the Father of the heavenly lights, who does not change like shifting shadows." I was so grateful for those dreams, for I did see them as gifts. But even more, I was extremely thankful I knew he was with us today and every day.

I looked back at Tommy as he finished his statement, wiping tears from his eyes. He glanced quickly toward Ron as he folded his paper and put it back into his pocket. Then he turned and walked back to his seat again, solemnly, looking at no one.

What was Ron thinking about Tommy's words? I noticed he'd composed himself and sat still, looking down toward the floor but facing the center of the room. And every so often, he'd look toward his family, his gaze never lingering there for long. *He appeared very disconnected from his family though*, I thought. In fact, I didn't see any eye contact between them. But maybe I was so overwhelmed by the emotion of the day, I couldn't tell.

My mind wandered for a brief moment and I thought of how different things might have been if only Jennifer and Jake had stayed together.

I remembered driving over to Mom's house a year or two before Jenny went missing. Parking my car in the driveway, I skipped up the stairs of the porch on a beautiful spring day. I was so eager to see Katie and Emma! Emma was still a baby, not quite a year old. There, at the top of the stairs near the far end of the porch, Jenny stood. She was leaning over the edge of the wooden porch rail. She looked engrossed in thought, and unhappy, as she took a sip from a soda can. She didn't even look at me, just stared downward over the rail toward the ground.

"Whatcha' doing, sis?" I spoke out, acting as if I didn't notice her mood.

"Not much. Waiting for Mom to get home," she replied. She sounded a million miles away.

"What are the girls doing?" I pushed, trying to get her to talk.

"Taking a nap."

"Oh," I said, sounding pretty neutral. A huge silence followed. She didn't seem to want to talk at all. Then she stared over toward the large elm tree in the front yard, avoiding my gaze.

"Are you okay, Jenn?" I asked. "I mean, if you want to talk about something, maybe you'll feel better," I coaxed.

"Nah, there's nothing anybody can do," she replied wistfully.

"Well…are you sure? You look kinda sad to me." I once again fished for an answer.

"It's just…Jake…I thought he'd get me a ring and we'd get married by now. But I guess he doesn't *want* to marry me," she blurted out emotionally and defensively.

"Oh. I see. I kind of thought you guys would have gotten married by now too," I bit my lip uncomfortably. I stood near her and leaned against the rail myself. "After all, you do have two little girls together. And I know you love him." My mind raced, trying to think of something to make her feel better. "You know, Jennifer, you deserve to be happy. And we all want you to be happy. But if he just doesn't want to get married, maybe this isn't the relationship for you. I can tell *you* want to get married.

Maybe he's just not ready to settle down, or he's thinking about it but hasn't decided for sure. Besides, I thought you two were going to the couples counseling at the new church you guys found?" I questioned. "It seemed like he was trying to make things work out. Are you still going?"

"Uh-huh. But I can tell he's not gonna buy me a ring. He never talks about us getting married," she spoke very softly, sullenly. Her disappointment was evident. And when she finally turned to look at me, she couldn't hide the sadness I saw in her eyes. She looked crushed! I wanted to make everything alright for her but knew I couldn't.

If only things could have been different…maybe Jennifer would still be here…her eventual breakup was so hard on her.

In the courtroom, it was now Mom's turn to give her victim impact statement, and I knew it would be extremely difficult for her to read it out loud. It was hard enough for her to write it, and knowing my mom, it would be even harder for her to read it with everyone listening and noticing the pain each word would bring. Still, she rose from her seat and made her way toward the judge's bench, sniffling and wiping her eyes with her tissue as she walked.

"Your Honor, I want to tell the court today that not only have I lost my daughter, I've lost my youngest child. She was only twenty years old and didn't deserve to be killed. She had her whole life ahead of her and had two small daughters who love her and will grow up not knowing her. She loved her daughters very much and would often spend her last dollar on them. Jennifer was a loving daughter, sister, and mother. Unless someone has had a child murdered, they cannot possibly know the heartache of losing one this way…" Her voice trailed off, and she paused, crying into her tissue again. Then calming herself, she finished reading her statement. "And I don't have anything else to say except, someday, Jennifer's killer will stand before a higher court and a higher judge, *the* supreme judge, God. And *then* he will get the punishment he *truly* deserves."

She was finished. I'd expected her to say more, but no. It was short and sweet, to the point. She didn't raise her voice. She didn't stare at him. She just sounded defeated. *Resigned.* I admired her calm, organized words, and knew I wouldn't have done as well if I'd been in her place. Finding her seat near Tommy, she sat down and welcomed the hugs of our family members sitting next to her. I reached forward from my seat and patted her shoulder from my seat on the bench behind her, telling her she did well.

"I love you, Mom," I reassured her, leaning forward and whispering to her. "It's okay…"

It was over…all but the final words from the judge. And I was relieved! I wanted to go somewhere away from all the sadness of the courtroom, just to get out of the building and go home. I wanted to let everything I'd heard sink in.

"Well, I think from what we've witnessed here today, we can walk away believing we've all heard a sincere apology. I do believe he's sorry for what he did," the judge stated, looking toward our family. Her compassionate smile conveyed the message, again, that she really cared about our pain. "And I hope both families can find peace and go on to live productive lives, knowing this day is behind you. This courtroom is adjourned," she ordered, as she slammed the gavel down on the bench.

We seemed to all stand at once. And then *I saw Tommy walk straight toward Ron's family, arms outstretched*! He was wiping tears away from his face, and everyone in Ron's family was crying. *And then, to our complete and utter amazement, Ron's mom said, "We want you to know…our tears aren't for him. They're for your family."*

What? I was *shocked!* The whole time we were in the courtroom, I thought they were crying for *Ron.* But they weren't. Apparently, they were extremely shocked he'd committed such a horrific crime and were not even going to show support for him on sentencing day.

Both families huddled together, crying and talking. Tommy and Mom gave Ron's mother a hug, and a moment later, she mentioned Jenny by name.

"I have Jennifer's picture on my refrigerator. She was so very pretty. And we're so sorry for what he's done," she apologized, wiping away her tears.

"Thank you. I appreciate that. But you guys have also lost someone in a way too," Tommy said. "You know, everybody lost in this whole situation. It's a sad thing for *all* of us."

I noticed various people in the courtroom watching our families talking and trying to comfort one another. I also knew most people wouldn't understand how two families brought together because of such a horrific crime and sitting on opposing sides of the courtroom could find any common ground, a reason to bond. But we had… and that bond was *grief.* There was no reason to hold his family responsible. They didn't kill Jennifer. And it appeared Ron's actions caused great pain for his family as well. If there was one thing our family understood, it was pain.

"Wow, Mary!" Shelba said, once we stepped outside the courtroom. "That was powerful, the way your family hugged and talked with Ron's family! The attorneys couldn't believe what they were seeing. It was incredible! I wish more families could be that compassionate toward each other."

"Yes, and it is pretty cathartic too. You know, I think God is pleased there are no hard feelings between our families. It helps both families to heal and feel some peace surrounding this awful situation. I know it meant a lot to my mom to have his mother tell her Jennifer's picture is on her refrigerator. She said she looks at it every day and prays for our family," I told her. "I couldn't imagine seeing the face, every day, of someone my own son had killed. Yet they do it. Those poor parents. God bless them! They have a lot to bear too."

"They sure do," she agreed. "Oh hey, Mr. Ackley wants to meet with you all for a minute and give you an apology letter from Ron. Did you know about that?"

"An apology letter? No, I hadn't heard he wrote one, but I'd love to have a copy," I answered, surprised at the sudden news.

I walked with her toward the victim witness center and found some of the others already there waiting. With my heart beating like a drum, I saw Ackley walk into the room shortly after us, carrying some papers. He approached Tommy and handed him the first copy then distributed copies to a few more members of our family. I took my copy and couldn't believe I was actually holding an apology from Jenny's killer. I looked over the handwriting, quickly, and then put it in my purse so I could read it later at home. I was exhilarated and thanked God for this unexpected surprise: an apology letter!

The rest of the day passed quickly, and a gentle numbness spread over me. We all had so much to take in and process. I felt an amazing peace flow all around me and noticed it seemed like a huge burden was removed. *Thank you for getting us through this day, Lord!* I prayed silently, knowing without him, it would have been so much more difficult.

Later I sat and read the letter from Ron to our family. It was pretty short. I'd been expecting more, something more emotional like we saw in the courtroom. Not quite a page long, it was also...well...awkward. It seemed he wanted to apologize but didn't exactly know how to go about it. He tried though. He said he was sorry for the pain we suffered because of our loss of Jennifer. And he said he was prepared to accept whatever the outcome would be, whether life in prison or death. There was an impressive section in the apology that really caught my attention, however. He stated he believed God chose his punishment. In fact, he said he believed God *intervened* in order for him to receive life without parole. Very interesting!

I found myself wondering if his belief in God was something he'd held within himself prior to killing Jennifer or if he'd acquired it while incarcerated. I realized I'd probably never know the answer and reminded myself it was truly between him and God.

"But, if he really believed God 'chose' his punishment, it shows he has a belief in God, right?" I asked myself out loud. I hoped, for his sake, he really did; and if he wasn't saved, it would lead him to the Lord. I also hoped he knew the passage in the Bible addressing repentance: "The Lord is not slow in keeping his promise, as some understand slowness. He is patient with you, not wanting anyone to perish, but everyone to come to repentance" (2 Peter 3:9 NIV). Either way, his punishment here on earth in this life was set. And he had a long time to think about repenting.

THE SENATOR PUSHES FORWARD

How quickly time sped by! I couldn't believe Thanksgiving 2007 had come and gone. And before I was even truly prepared, the Christmas season approached. It would be another Christmas without Jennifer, the third since her death. We knew what to expect though, the sadness of her absence and the memories of Christmases past *with her*. I still felt blessed. In fact, I felt closer to God during the past year than ever before. Just knowing he answered so many prayers, so many *monumental* prayers, was incredible! He proved to me over and over again he hears our cries and cares for us. So I couldn't help wondering what the New Year would bring. How would God keep showing his care for our family? Would he still know the desires of our hearts? I knew...I believed he would, and I continued to pray and talk with him.

"Lord, thank you for just instilling the patience within me each time I've prayed for your help," I told God. "I know I have to always be willing to wait for your answers."

Patience has never been one of my strong points, but I was learning with God, it really is mandatory. Plus it helps to simply being aware of his leading. Paying attention to my dreams and trying to understand their meaning in his eyes was important. Memories of past dreams involving other deceased loved ones flickered through my mind. I was realizing possibly some of them were (also) a kind of wonderful contact God allowed. I was so thankful the Lord gave those great visits to me. It made me feel so incredibly special! I wanted to share them with others and made a mental note to call my friend Sheila and talk with her about them.

It was December already, and the eighth day brought a bitter cold wind and major change to Oklahoma. A massive Arctic cold front descended upon the state, freezing everything within its path. Frigid precipitation in the form of ice, snow, and sleet pounded the roads, paralyzing travelers as they slid haphazardly along highways and side streets in an attempt to reach their destinations. I couldn't remember a time when I'd seen so many broken trees, split in two, lying in streets and yards. And an unbelievable number of homes and businesses were without power. Oh, the joys of winter in Oklahoma! After many long weeks of cleanup, the community accomplished their task. Neighbor helped neighbor, and eventually, even the landscape regained its former tidy appearance. Thank heavens people in our state pull together in tough times. *Just another reason to feel blessed,* I thought to myself. *Oklahoma really is a great state!*

"I'm so excited!" I told Sheila during a weekend phone call. "I can't believe he's actually working on getting a new law passed. And he's even going to try to have them name it *Jenny's law.* Isn't that awesome?" I asked my best friend excitedly over the phone. We were barely into the month of February, and I was ecstatic over the wonderful news I'd recently gotten from Senator Reynolds. He'd been hard at work since I first spoke to him through e-mail, regarding the new law we wanted so badly for our state. I had a great feeling 2008 was going to be just as great a year as the last.

"Yes, that's incredible!" she agreed. "I'm so glad you pursued this. When will you find out for sure?"

"Well, I believe the legislative session ends in May, so it'll be awhile. It's going to be *so* hard waiting until then, though." I imagined the next three months feeling like *years*. Thank heavens Sheila was there to listen while I repeated myself again and again. I knew she must be thinking I sounded like a broken record. Our talks always turned toward our hopes for the new law. But she stayed positive, helping me keep perspective while being my shoulder to lean on.

As it turned out, the waiting wasn't as difficult as I thought it might be. After all, I had my job to keep me focused. And I was also delightfully surprised when I was asked to represent crime victims at a seminar to be held during National Crime Victims' Rights Week in April, presented by Oklahoma City University and the Oklahoma State Bureau of Investigations. This seminar would be the Second Annual Victimology Seminar.

"So what does the victim representative do at the seminar?" I e-mailed my friend Robbie, who worked for the Oklahoma Department of Corrections. She was the contact person who actually mentioned my name to the OSBI.

"Oh, it's kind of a panel-type thing, for one. You'll be there to observe some of what the criminal investigative process is like, plus you'll be able to present to the attendees at the seminar a little of what the victim perspective is like during and after a violent crime. And if you have questions about the investigative process, they'll be able to give you some insight in to that as well. I've already talked with the contact person and told them your family lost someone to murder," she explained.

"Sounds good. Do I need to bring anything or do anything beforehand?" I asked.

"Nope, just bring yourself," she replied. "Oh, and I'll need you to send me a bio so they'll have it for their brochures or whatever they pass out to attendees. I'll just e-mail it on to them if you want to e-mail me one. But I'll be in touch with you before that week, since I'm working on the brochure for the ceremony at the capitol for Crime Victims' Rights Day again this year. By the way, you wouldn't want to be a speaker for that ceremony on April 16 as well, would you?" she asked. "You could talk a little about trying to get *Jenny's law* passed, if you wanted. It would be a great opportunity to get the word out."

"I'm definitely going to be there," I typed back to her with a smiley face at the end of the sentence. "And yes, that'd be really cool!" I responded enthusiastically. "I'd *love* to speak that day! Just let me know for sure and I'll get something written up."

"Okay, great! Go ahead and plan to do it and I'll check back, but I can almost guarantee you can be one of the speakers. There'll probably be two or three victim representatives who'll speak," she answered. "This could be your chance to get some of the legislators on board with *Jenny's law.*"

I read the excitement in the tone of her e-mail and knew she really wanted this new law to pass too. After all, she was a crime victim herself. Having lost her own mother at the hands of a murderer, she was probably one of the biggest supporters of crime victims' rights I'd met.

I couldn't agree *more* about getting the word out to as many legislators as possible too. Brief scenarios of different ways to present my speech at the capitol flitted through my mind. I imagined my speech eliciting a strong interest from the listener, actually making them want *Jenny's law* in our state. I had just under two months to get a speech prepared and couldn't believe I was going to have such a great opportunity to get the word out. I just hoped people in "high" places could see the importance of having this law in Oklahoma. I knew God would be there with me. So there was no point in worrying about it. God already knew the outcome.

I turned my attention back to the paperwork on my desk and sorted through the remaining items I needed to finish before I left work for the day.

I had my new "work" cut out for me! After hearing from Robbie that I would indeed be one of the speakers at the capitol on Crime Victims' Rights Day, I raced against the clock to get everything written I wanted to say. I wanted to convey to the listeners, first and foremost, the empty, sad feeling experienced by a homicide family member and just how drastically it changes them. I wanted them to understand the emotional devastation we all experience when someone we love is brutally struck down and torn out of this world, torn out of our very lives.

So I wrote and rewrote my speech, finally calling it "A Day in the Life of a Homicide Survivor." It was difficult to write, to say the least. Painful memories of those initial weeks following her burial brought back to mind the sharp, heart-wrenching pain we'd grown accustomed to. But the observers needed to hear and understand what we went through. I only prayed there'd be a lot of legislators there to hear it.

I read over again what I'd written. The speech started with a description of what it's like to wake up *every* morning and realize a loved one is dead, murdered, and not coming back. Then it progressed to the fact no matter what one does throughout the day, something triggers the mind to keep remembering the dead loved one. This initially happens many, many times a day and is something you cannot stop. Finally, toward the end, I described the vain attempts to rest and sleep at the end of the day. What may or may not happen, though, is the dreaming… about your loved one. And I mentioned whether I did or didn't dream about her, sleep was seldom restful. The grief seemed to invade even the sleeping hours.

"I think that'll work," I told myself as I put the final touches on the speech. But somehow, it still seemed incomplete. It needed something more at the end.

I wonder if I could find the right poem, a poem that evokes the empty feeling I want them to understand, I thought to myself. I suddenly remembered one that could be a good choice and plugged in a search for it on my computer. It was one I'd heard once in a movie. And I just couldn't imagine *not* ending my speech with a beautiful poem to catch their attention and their emotions. This one might work.

"Yes….this is it!" I told myself triumphantly, staring at the author's name. I quickly scanned over the words of the poem. Would they truly be suitable? Appropriate? I believed they would, and decided to read "Stop All the Clocks" (W.H. Auden) at the end of my speech.

Although it was apparent the poem was written about the death of a mate, its message could apply to anyone who's lost someone to death. It accurately describes the strong emotion felt after the death of a loved one, the sadness and feeling of loss. How appropriate for homicide survivors! How many of us have lost weight, our appetites, or our interest in common everyday activities after our loss due to the murder of a loved one? The answer is *probably just about everyone who's lost someone to murder.* It is an indescribably desperate feeling. I couldn't imagine not having the Lord to lean on.

Hearing the *World News* signing off for the evening on the living room TV, I realized I was a little behind schedule. Six o'clock already! Emma was probably hopping around, looking out the window and waiting for me to pick her up. It was her turn to spend the night, and she wasn't a very patient little girl. Thank heavens I had the day off and could get a few things done before she came over to spend some time with me.

"If I can just get this computer shut down and put away now without being interrupted," I thought, hoping I could get into my car before Emma tried to track me down.

Rrrrrring! Rrrrrring! I couldn't believe the timing of those girls.

I bet I can guess who that *is calling*, I thought as I walked toward the ringing phone and read the name on the caller ID. "Yep, I knew it!" I said to myself with a laugh. I answered it anyway.

"Aunt KayKay? Are you on your way to pick me up?" I heard from the small voice on the other end.

AN ANGEL DISGUISED AS A DETECTIVE

I checked my e-mail frequently, looking for the response I hoped for from Senator Reynolds. Although he kept in touch, letting us know he drafted a bill a few months earlier, which made desecration of a corpse a crime, he was still trying to convince others in the senate the new law needed to be passed. It seemed they weren't all so eager to have it in Oklahoma. In fact, we actually heard there was a lawmaker who stated there were *"too many criminal laws already in Oklahoma,"* and our family just needed to *"heal and move on."* It came as quite a shock since it was never our family's desire to have the law passed because we weren't healed or hadn't moved forward. The whole point of the law would be to hold the murderer accountable for the crimes committed against the victim's body after death, crimes that impeded the investigation and sometimes kept the family from claiming the body due to the destruction of the body and evidence. I couldn't help but wonder how the lawmaker would have felt if it were *their* sister who'd been burned beyond recognition and went unidentified for eight months.

I was deflated and started worrying. No matter how I tried to stay focused on the positive, doubt crept in. How could anyone think *any state* shouldn't have a law against a crime like Jenny's? I gave myself pep talks and fought against negative thoughts. Plus I reminded myself of all the prayers God answered in our family regarding Jennifer's death. Surely he would see to it that our senator was able to convince his colleagues to support this law. I just couldn't imagine any other outcome.

"Maybe you just need to quit worrying about it," my dad would say when I'd express my concerns to him. He was right, after all. I knew worrying didn't make outcomes any different. Besides, I also knew what the Bible said about worry:

"Can any one of you by worrying add a single hour to your life?" (NIV Matthew 6:27). The answer is, of course, no.

However, the Bible does state something is to be gained by trusting in God:

"May the God of hope fill you with all joy and peace as you trust in him, so that you may overflow with hope by the power of the Holy Spirit" (NIV Romans 15:13).

It was simple. All I had to do was trust God to fill me with hope. He would do the rest. How hard it is for humans to do this, most of the time. We want to control our little worlds in every area. And as I've learned many times before, it isn't always possible. Instead, we have to simply pray for God to fill us with hope.

Making a mental note to do just that, I reminded myself this was no different than wanting to find Jennifer's killer. I would be patient, keep praying and hoping God would deliver. As a result, I believed he would give me peace.

While I worked on maintaining hope, it seemed God was working on people's hearts. Toward the end of February, I received an inspiring e-mail from the forensic detective who recreated Jennifer's likeness. I was elated! She'd been talking to others about our dream for *Jenny's law* and wanted me to know she'd been in contact with the senator too. She even attached a copy of an e-mail she sent to him in support of the new law we wanted passed.

The e-mail stated she and other professionals in her field of work supported and wanted the proposed law because they "work with these cases every day." She also wrote, "We are touched by these individuals through their deaths." Her support seemed truly heartfelt, stating the law would help the professionals who "have to see and physically deal with the torture administered to the body after the ultimate sacrifice of death." And the most powerful statement she made drove home our point: "To kill someone is looked at as the ultimate crime, but to dismember, destroy and eliminate a person from existing after they have been torn out of the world needs to be addressed and punished as well." She understands the pain families suffer when their loved one's bodies are destroyed. And from what she'd written in the e-mail, it was clear the professionals who work with the desecrated bodies are emotionally affected as well. God bless her! I was so grateful she put that into words.

Scrolling down toward the bottom of the e-mail, I noticed she included pictures of Jennifer. One of the pictures was of her as a teenager taken a few years before she died. The others were of her reconstructed head. It was evident they were all shown together in order to compare and show the similarities, revealing the fact the reconstruction *was* very similar to pictures of Jennifer. Wow! What a great job she'd done. Just seeing them in the e-mail reminded me of the moment I saw her reconstruction on television the afternoon in August of 2006. The similarities were so striking!

I couldn't wait to contact the detective and let her know how much her e-mail to the senator meant to me and our family. Tilting back in my office chair for a moment, I wondered if I should call her now or e-mail her. I definitely wouldn't want to bother her, especially at work. There's no doubt she'd be extremely busy, possibly helping another family by working on their loved one's reconstruction. Not wanting to interrupt her, I finally decided to call later in the day and reached toward the mouse to close out the e-mail. However, I found myself staring at the colorful pictures of Jenny once more, stretched across the monitor.

I miss you so much, Jennifer, I thought to myself. *If you could just know people care about what happened to you. Maybe not all of them do. But there are many.*

I felt my spirit lift and thought about the e-mail I'd just received. I shouldn't be feeling down. After all, the e-mail was a great sign. It meant *Jenny's law* had gained more backing than we realized. And just knowing we had support from people who understood what her body suffered meant a lot. Hopefully, if those people cared and voiced their opinion, others might do the same.

Later in the evening, I called and talked about the e-mail with Mom. She was thrilled our forensic detective was voicing her support for the new law.

"Did you talk to her, or just get a copy of the e-mail?" she asked.

"I called her back when I took my afternoon break," I answered. "And she was actually happy to talk to me for a few moments. She said she'd been thinking about our family a lot, wondering how we were doing."

"Well…isn't that nice of her?" my mom exclaimed. She'd really liked the detective when she first met her during a news conference around the time Jenny was identified. And she never forgot Traci worked hard to get permission for Jennifer to be buried with the reconstruction.

"Yes, it is," I agreed. "She's really a nice person. I'm so glad she's the one who did Jennifer's reconstruction. I can't believe she's taking the time and trouble to send Senator Reynolds an e-mail to ask him to push on for the law."

"Oh. Hey, before I forget…," Mom started. "Did Emma bring a little watch to your house the last time she came over? She can't find it. It's a little pink one with princesses on the watch band."

"Uh, no. I don't think so," I replied. "I haven't seen one lying around. I'll look a little more when we get off the phone though," I promised. "But I wanted to tell you something while we're talking on the phone anyway. After Emma went home last time, I found the sweetest little poem that either she or Katie wrote. It's pretty sad, Mom. I guess it must have been Katie who wrote it since Emma doesn't write very well yet."

"What's it say?" she wanted to know.

"Well, let's see. It's kind of hard to read, in that little kid 'chicken scratch.' Know what I mean? I'll give it a try though," I said. Taking a deep breath, I read aloud from the paper I'd found lying on the dining room table: "I miss my mommy so much. She died and lives in the sky in heaven now. I love you Mommy!" That was all, short and sweet. Six-year-olds write what they feel, that's for sure.

I noticed there was nothing but silence on the other end of the phone.

"Mom? Did you hear it?" I asked.

She sniffled and then finally responded, "Yes. I heard it. It's just sad a little child would be writing something like that. Breaks my heart! They shouldn't *be* missing their mom. She should be here."

"Yes…I know," I replied. "I wish we could bring her back for them. They'll always miss her because they'll always miss having a mom, period. You know, you'll always miss having your daughter and I'll always miss having my little sister. But they'll always miss having a mother. I just hate that! I know Jennifer wouldn't want them grieving and being sad. But I just don't know how to help them *not* feel the emptiness of missing her. And it doesn't help they don't have a father in their lives, either."

"Well, we just have to be the next best thing. At least they have aunts who love them and a grandmother who's always there for them," she said. "Plus their Grandpa Tommy sees them every time he's able to come back here."

I agreed with her. I just hoped and prayed they knew how much they were loved. Surrounded by family, they appeared to be thriving. They were active, happy little girls who wanted to experience everything in a day, just like most kids. I couldn't wait to teach them how to roller blade, like I did their mom, or to ride bikes. In fact, Katie already had a small bike with training wheels that I kept at my house for her. She was just afraid to take the training wheels off. But soon she'd be ready, and I couldn't wait to help her when she was.

April quietly arrived, and I excitedly anticipated *Crime Victims' Rights Week 2008.* I received a copy of the week's schedule from my friend Robbie and couldn't believe the number of activities lined up, nearly one every day of that week somewhere in our state.

Yes! Let's have a strong week for crime victims' rights! I thought as I looked over the schedule, wanting to somehow make a difference in our state for the better regarding crime. Grabbing a highlighter, I marked the events I wanted to attend.

To kick off the beginning of the week, I attended my first event, an outdoor candlelight vigil held at the capitol. Scheduled for Sunday evening (April 13) the turnout was relatively small, and a slight breeze blowing from the north put just a hint of a chill in the air. But the spirit of the event was strong, bringing broken hearts together in a unified observance of the affect violent crime has on families. I recognized several of the attendees and was thrilled to read on the agenda a solo was being sung by Susie, a very caring and compassionate victim advocate I'd met at the homicide seminar. Someone told me she had a beautiful voice, but the rumors didn't even do her justice. When I heard her, the voice was, in a word, *angelic.*

It was the words of the song that were most touching though, reaching into the hearts of our small crowd. The melancholy tune and comforting message they conveyed commanded the attention of each person as we stood there at the south entrance of the capitol. I noticed tear-filled eyes throughout our small turnout and reminded myself to not become too emotional. After all, I knew where Jennifer was and she was with God, safe and free of any pain. God wouldn't want me grieving uncontrollably for her, but I felt certain he'd understand my missing her deeply.

Speaker after speaker, I listened. They were wonderful, compassionate people who understood the needs of the crime victim community, a district attorney from a neighboring county, the first assistant district attorney from my own county—Scott—and several homicide survivors. They were *all* affected and changed by the crimes they dealt with in their everyday lives, either as a family member or through their work in the community.

Short and sweet, the vigil closed with a special "circle of strength," which involved everyone standing in a circle and holding a small lit candle. One by one, we took turns stating who we were there to remember. I felt a lump form in my throat, acting as a road block, when it was my turn to speak. I could barely get it out, half whispering Jennifer's name. After all, saying her name there just made her death even more real. I tried to redirect my thoughts to shut down the painful emotions. But it didn't work well either because I looked directly across the circle and saw the same sadness in the eyes of friends who shared in the painful reminder their loved ones were gone too.

What an awful group to be a member of. I wished none of us had a reason to attend this type of event.

I tried switching to thoughts of different family members, wondering what they were all doing right now. I'd told my mom and Tommy about this special week, but Mom wasn't big on attending events. And I figured Tommy, like me, would be involved with something to remember crime victims this week in California. I hoped and prayed they were all healing from the shock of Jennifer's death and aware God's love was healing each one of our lives.

As the group was breaking up and leaving, I studied their expressions once more. Slowly they walked toward their cars. They were mostly people who'd lost someone to homicide. Still, everyone was smiling and chatting with each other as they walked. They actually appeared to be reasonably happy. However, I imagined the homicide families gracefully hiding their pain like me. And I felt certain their happiness had a boundary, a limit. It was almost like we all wore a mask, the same mask. It was a mask of invisible sadness, the one with deep cuts that refused to completely mend.

The morning of April 16, 2008, I read and reread my speech. More than just a little nervous, I practiced my approach, hoping I didn't come across too bold, too timid, or too jittery. The day had arrived, *the* day I'd get to announce to the public our family's desire for a new law in Oklahoma. I hoped all who attended would agree it was an important one for our state.

The ceremony, which was to be held inside the capitol, was scheduled for 1:00 p.m. Being overly paranoid about being late for anything, I pulled into the parking lot forty-five minutes early and checked the ringer volume on my cell phone. A ringing phone during the ceremony would not be a good idea! I grabbed my notes, silenced the ringer, and headed toward the building, passing through the security check point near the entrance.

Yeah, I'm ahead of time, I noted silently as I found the event area, the rotunda. I couldn't help noticing I wasn't the only early bird. Several people I recognized stood near a table by the podium, picking up square plastic lapel buttons. I noticed each bore the National Crime Victims' Rights Week logo, so I picked up a couple of them. "Justice for victims, justice for all" was printed in bold black-and-white lettering, catching the attention of most who passed by the table.

"Hey, I made it here early, like you!" My friend Lena called out and waved at me as she walked toward the table. Her always cheery voice was positive and uplifting, and I felt myself smiling and feeling more confident than I actually was.

"Yes, and I'm nervous!" I answered with a small laugh. "I hope I don't pass out and fall down just as they ask me to come up to the podium and speak. Wouldn't that be awful? I get my chance to make a plea for *Jenny's law*, and all I can do is pass out?" I laughed again, wondering if laughter could help ease the jitters I felt wrecking my insides.

"Well, you'll do just fine," she encouraged me.

"I'm pretty nervous, but I think I'll be okay," I agreed. "I just want to be sure people understand how difficult it is to function after someone you love is killed. Plus having somebody destroy the body afterwards, to hide evidence…it's monstrous! It just can't be okay to *not* have a law against this."

Feeling agitated, I thought of all our family experienced since Jenny disappeared and was found. I took out a few of the buttons I brought to the event myself, buttons with Jenny's smiling face on a bright red background along with her birth date and murder date. Somberly, I arranged them on the table next to the square ones for victims' rights week. I hoped lots of people would want one, and I wore one on the lapel of my own black cotton jacket. Lena watched as I arranged and rearranged the buttons, trying to assure myself they looked perfect.

"Well, here's a hug for good luck, but I know you don't need it," she said softly as she gently squeezed my shoulders. "You're doing something that needs to be done, for many more families down the road. Just believe God's already making it happen, and get up to the podium and get the word out."

Watching her walk to her seat, I thought about her encouragement and knew she was right. God already knew whether or not the law would be passed. I just needed to do my part today and leave it in God's hands. I imagined him standing near the back of the rotunda, rooting me on. The whole room would be overtaken with his presence, so how could I go wrong? Yes, I could *do* this.

What seemed like mere moments passed, and the room was nearly filled with people! Fold-up chairs were lined neatly in rows, seating members from our homicide support group, their family members, and a few other people I recognized from other parts of our state who had a loved one murdered. Microphones were checked for sound quality, and before I knew it, the master of ceremonies, prominent local lawyer Mike Turpen, introduced himself and addressed the crowd.

I was impressed with the display of support for crime victims. In fact, during the opening of the program, we were all pleasantly surprised when many of the legislators, who happened to be in the capitol, introduced themselves one by one to the entire group of attendees. It was the perfect way to get the event started!

Soon the ceremony was underway, and although I knew there'd be other crime victims attending and speaking, nothing prepared me for the sadness of the story given by the speaker just ahead of me. He'd lost a six-month-old baby daughter, drowned in a bathtub, because she'd been left unattended while her mother slept in another room. I couldn't imagine the heartache he'd suffered! Even though his daughter wasn't intentionally killed, she was neglected and died as a result. Amazingly enough, he was able to get the definition of the term "child neglect" modified, according to Oklahoma law, and as a result the "Letha Kay Louise Slate act" was passed. This meant even though a child had all the food, shelter, medical care, and proper clothing they needed, if there was a lack of supervision, a person could be charged with the murder of a child. In Letha's case, her mother was only charged with manslaughter and given a four-year prison sentence. But what a victory for Letha's dad and for other similar cases! He made a *change* and such a *major* one! It was just more proof that laws could be created, instigated by crime victims.

Encouraged by the story I'd just heard, I shuffled through my notes and prepared to give my speech.

Lord, please don't let me mess this up, I prayed silently.

Hearing my name called, I walked to the podium. It was time. As I looked around the room, I couldn't help noticing everyone's attention was focused on me and what I had to say. I could have heard a pin drop. It was that quiet.

I started reading my notes. So far so good. I read on about what a homicide survivor's day is like, just as I'd rehearsed. Everything flowed. Nervously, I kept looking around the room, hoping to see Senator Reynolds. How I hoped he could make it to the ceremony to hear what I'd written about him presenting *Jenny's law* to the senate! Disappointedly, I realized he wasn't there.

Oh well, I thought. *He couldn't make it here. The important thing is that he's working on it. The fact he's not here doesn't mean he isn't pushing for the law.* I knew he was aware of the ceremony because I'd contacted his secretary days before and told her to be sure and remind him. I refocused on the papers in front of me and kept reading despite the nervous shaking of my fingers.

"…So let's not give up, give in, or turn away from the tyranny of crime in Oklahoma. Let's meet it head-on. Let's make some important changes one day at a time and one law at a time. Thank you," I read from the last few lines in my speech.

Applause filled the room, and I glanced toward the ceremonies announcer. Five minutes. That's approximately how long it took for me to read my speech. But was it enough? Did it capture the audience attention? Would people support *Jenny's law*?

"Hey, good job!" Mr. Turpen stated in a quiet voice with a nod and a smile. "You can go ahead and have a seat."

"Thank you," I responded, walking back to my seat near the front row.

Whew! You did it! You're finished! I thought as a smile crept over my face. And I did it without freezing up, stuttering or sneezing! I was amazed I hadn't slipped up.

Filled with relief, I soaked in the remainder of the ceremony, thankful to be able to share my desire for *Jenny's law* with others. Still, I couldn't help wondering if any of the legislators who introduced themselves at the beginning of the ceremony heard what I said about *Jenny's law.* How I hoped they did! And I wondered if the lieutenant governor knew about it before today. I noticed her watching me and listening while I spoke. Surely she did. Knowing very little about the passage of laws in our state, I wasn't sure exactly *who* would be aware. All I knew was that I wanted *everyone* to want this law.

As the ceremony ended, I made a point to give some of the lapel buttons to those who attended, including Mike Turpen and Lieutenant Governor Jari Askins. They both graciously accepted, immediately pinning them on their clothes.

"Thank you so much for wearing my sister's button," I told the lieutenant governor. "I just hope people realize how much we need this law in Oklahoma."

With a sympathetic smile, she gave me a hug and softly responded, "I'm hearing good things about *Jenny's law.* So don't give up hope!"

It was just the positive feedback I was looking for! She was aware of the action taken by the senator to create *Jenny's law* and apparently thought it had a chance. I was thrilled she shared the information with me and knew I must have glowed with happiness and relief a few moments later when I had my picture taken with her. What a fantastic way to end the observance of crime victims' rights week at the capitol! I only wished Mom, Tommy, and my siblings could have attended. Between work, doctor appointments, and of course distance, it just wasn't possible for them to make it.

It was time to go. With a final glance around the room and toward the podium where I'd stood, I said my goodbyes and walked out of the capitol. I'd done everything I could to spread the news about *Jenny's law*, and I exited the building with a sense of renewed hope. With every other prayer answered by God, I couldn't imagine him letting us down now.

The following day arrived quickly, and I anxiously drove to the Oklahoma City University campus for the Second Annual Victimology Seminar. Although I'd known for weeks I'd be attending, I also knew I wouldn't be making any speeches. I'd be there primarily as a "voice" for crime victims, so I'd be on a panel and probably would be asked my views regarding some crime issues. No need for notes. Yeah! I couldn't wait! It was another chance to get the word out about *Jenny's law*, and I wanted it to get as much exposure as possible.

Walking briskly across a neatly manicured section of the lush green campus lawn, I found the building I needed and processed through the registration. I was barely through the registration line when I glanced behind me and noticed our very own forensic detective signing in for the same seminar. I couldn't believe it! The detective who created Jennifer's reconstruction was standing not six feet from me!

Wow, thank you, God! I praised inwardly. *I have to talk to her.*

I patiently waited until she cleared the registration line and then stepped forward and caught her attention.

"Traci?" I blurted out questioningly.

"Yes," she stated half questioningly. Her expression conveyed she had no idea who I was.

"Hi. My name is Mary, and I'm Jennifer's sister," I said nervously. All of a sudden I felt tongue tied! "Uh…I mean, my sister is the young lady that you did the reconstruction on…Jennifer…I talked to you on the phone a while back about the email you sent Senator Reynolds…?"

"Oh, right. Yes! Wow, it's nice to meet you in person!" she replied enthusiastically. "How have you been? And your family?" she took my hand.

"Pretty good…considering. If it hadn't been for your recreation of Jenny's face, we'd be worse." I gave a small nervous laugh.

"Well, I'm glad I could help." She was clearly concerned yet relieved.

"Hey, do you think I could talk with you after the seminar is over? I mean…I guess I'm just a little curious about how that whole process works and how you were able to get the reconstruction so close to what she actually looked like." I hoped I wasn't being a pest.

"Sure! We can talk afterwards. Just holler before you get ready to leave," she agreed.

"Great!" I replied. "I'll catch you later then."

She walked away, and I almost pinched myself. I couldn't believe she was here, and I couldn't wait to talk with her after the seminar.

The afternoon was packed with incredible information from police investigations to domestic violence presentations. And just being able to assist law enforcement by supplying a few victim perspectives was empowering for me. I regretted the event coming to a close toward the end of the afternoon but understood the honor I'd been given by being asked to attend.

"Wow, that was really interesting, wasn't it?" I asked Traci as we walked around the campus, looking for a bench to sit on while we chatted afterwards.

“Yes, they put a lot into it, that’s for sure,” she agreed. “And I’m glad I came. I’m glad you came too. It’s got to be pretty tough for you still dealing with what happened to Jennifer.” She gazed across the lawn, obviously thinking about Jenny’s death, and we finally found the perfect spot, a shady area facing several gorgeous redbud trees in full bloom.

“Yes, it is, but at least we know where her body is now,” I answered. “By the way, you have *no* idea how much it meant to our family to be able to bury her with that reconstruction. She deserved to at least be buried with a face.”

“I agree. I just hate it that your family had to deal with what the killer did, burning her body and all. That’s just evil!” she exclaimed. “And even though those components are very expensive, my boss totally understood your family’s request. We’re glad we could do that for you guys.”

Sitting quietly for several seconds, we both let our conversation slowly sink in until Traci broke the silence and asked me the question I’d wanted to ask *her*.

“So you were wondering how I was able to make the reconstruction look so much like Jennifer?” she asked me.

“Yes. It was amazing!” I excitedly burst out. “When I first saw her on TV that August, I saw her from the angle showing mostly her right side, kind of a partial profile. It looked *just like* her jaw line, her nose, her eyes, everything. I couldn’t believe it. I knew it was *her* the moment I saw it. In fact, I’m the one who called my sister Jackie and told her to turn the TV on and watch the broadcast. How could you make it so accurate without having her picture to guide you?” I wanted to know.

"Well, I know this is going to sound strange, but I really felt like she was there *with* me, guiding and helping me. I know it sounds weird, but I couldn't have made it look like her without some kind of help. Maybe it was God guiding me, or her. I don't know. But, I do know it wasn't just me. All I had to work with was her basic bone structure, her skull. The extra subtleties were something I couldn't have come up with on my own, like the exact shape of her nose. I truly believe I had some kind of spiritual guidance."

"Ah! I wondered about that. You know you have a really awesome way of helping families. It's a gift. The fact you helped *our* family is incredible, but you've probably helped others and will continue to help even more. And I absolutely believe God is behind it all. You were meant to create her accurate likeness."

I paused, looking away from Traci toward the splash of purplish red color emanating from the trees nearby. I felt emotional again and wondered if it would ever change when I thought of Jenny's death.

"Yes, I agree. I think so too. And I think your push for the new law is very important, as you probably noticed from the e-mail I sent the senator. It's sad someone has to clean and prepare a destroyed body part so family can identify them. It's emotionally painful for us too," she said.

"I can see it *would* be. Man, it's so sad there are people in the world who think nothing of doing something so savage to another person," I replied wistfully.

We sat, together, letting all we'd just shared sink in. Though I knew I'd love to hear more about her work, I didn't want to press her. I glanced down at my watch and noticed it was later than I'd realized. Bummer! We'd been talking nearly forty minutes and I had errands to run on my way home.

"Hey, Traci, I've gotta scoot," I hurriedly told her. "But I've really enjoyed our talk. I hope I see you again sometime before long, maybe another seminar someday, huh?" I smiled as I made my apologies, and she looked surprised as she also quickly glanced at *her* watch.

"Wow, it *is* getting late. I enjoyed our talk too! And tell your mom and Tommy I said hello, okay?" she asked.

"Okay, Traci, I will. And thanks again for all you do to help people. God bless you in your work!" I gave her a quick hug.

I sprinted quickly to my car, started it up, and headed toward the post office. I didn't want to get there after they closed. Thinking over the past several hours while I drove, I couldn't believe the way Traci and I just "happened" to be at the same seminar. After all, it wasn't like there were hundreds of police detectives attending. There weren't really many, maybe forty to fifty people maximum attending the entire seminar. Was it coincidence maybe? I don't think so. I didn't believe in coincidence anymore. There were too many things falling into place for me to ever again believe they were not connected somehow. And I believed God was responsible for the connecting.

OKLAHOMA GAINS *JENNY'S LAW*

With the month of April behind me, I hoped and prayed May would bring the passage of *Jenny's law.* One thing May definitely brought, even though no one wanted it, was more violent spring storms. May first arrived quietly enough and then turned into a raging weather monster later in the evening that brought with it hail the size of baseballs, pounding and tearing into everything in its path.

"Man! Why does everything seem to happen in our neighborhood?" I asked one of my neighbors in frustration as we stood outside, surveying the damage to our homes. We got hit hard!

"I don't know," Don replied. "But I'm surprised we weren't hit by another tornado. They seem to love central Oklahoma, and the conditions were perfect."

"Wow! I'm pretty sure I'll have to get a new roof. And my skylight is busted out," I complained.

"Join the club! You know what they say. If you don't like the weather in Oklahoma, just wait awhile. It'll change in five minutes." Smiling, he pointed up to the sky and looked toward the now calm, white fluffy clouds.

"Yep, you're right about that!" I finally laughed. "I guess the weather can't be all sunshine and roses. At least it wasn't an earthquake, right? And we still have our houses." Despite my laughter though, I was grumbling inside. Man! What a pounding mother nature dished out lately! My thoughts drifted back to the ice storm of last winter, and I was amazed at the damage then and still wondered how much more people in this state could take. It seemed it was always *something*, some weather extreme to keep people shaking their heads and digging into their pockets for more repairs, more replacements, more, more, more.

Even though I was frustrated because I'd now have to deal with my insurance company and a roofing company, I tried to stay optimistic. I thanked God I still *had* a house standing when so many people lost homes due to tornadoes. Plus, I couldn't afford to think negatively when we were so close to finding out whether or not the new law would pass. After all, the end of the legislative session was only a few weeks away. We'd either be elated or extremely disappointed. If I could just keep everything in perspective…not get too bummed out if the law didn't get passed. After all, the most important thing was we *did* get to bury Jennifer.

Keeping in frequent contact with Senator Reynolds's secretary, I tried to find out as much as possible about the progress of the bill. However, the information I got wasn't all good. As it turned out, the original bill was shot down, rejected. There was just not enough support for the bill to stand by itself.

I didn't have to wait for long though. Only days after getting the news that the bill wouldn't go through, I received the e-mail that gave me major hope! It seemed one of the other senators was going to attach the language of *Jenny's law* on to one of *his* bills. I was thrilled and couldn't wait to let my family know. There was a chance it might still happen! Although it would be incorporated into another bill as a section of that bill, it could possibly still pass once it was placed on the agenda for the senate. I wanted to jump up and down and hug Senator Reynolds's secretary for giving me the news but thanked her instead in an e-mail. Besides, it wasn't a done deal just yet. It was only May 13, 2008, and we still had ten days until the end of the legislative session. I was still not certain it would pass…

Days later, I could hardly concentrate! I knew I'd hear something soon and wanted to know the moment it happened. There were only three days left until it was official, one way or another. How on earth could I keep my mind on anything else?

I'll put a few more insurance calls into the computer and then check my e-mail, I thought to myself as I looked at the clock on my desk. *I'm sure there's nothing new yet.*

To my delight, there *was* an e-mail. Short and sweet, it was verification from Senator Reynolds's office that he was still going to have the new law called *Jenny's law* if it passed. Fantastic! It was a great indication that he was working hard to get it passed *and* to honor the memory of my sister. Woo-hoo! *Only three more days…*

The morning of Friday, May 23, 2008, was nerve wracking!

"Make sure you call me as soon as you hear something, okay?" Mom requested. It was barely 9:00 a.m., and she was calling me at work, making sure I didn't forget to call and let her know whether or not the bill passed.

"I will, Mom. I promise. I don't know if it'll be morning or afternoon. I might not even know anything until Monday. It depends on what time they finish up today," I said. "Trust me, though, I'll contact you and Tommy as soon as I hear something."

I waited, then I waited some more. And just when I decided it wouldn't happen, *it did!* Shortly before leaving work for the day at 4:00 p.m., I got the e-mail from the senator's office, stating the new bill containing a section for *Jenny's law* overwhelmingly passed! Exhilarated, I popped up from my desk and gave a yelp. I was stunned!

Oh my gosh! I have to tell somebody! I thought as I raced around my desk.

To my extreme joy, I didn't have long to wait because a few moments later several of my coworkers came through the office. I could barely contain my excitement as I shared the great news with them. My boss was told next and then a close friend several offices down the hall. Hands shaking, I called Mom and Tommy.

"I had a feeling it would pass!" Mom said exuberantly. "Anyone who heard it wasn't against the law *before* was shocked. I'm so relieved!"

"Awesome! We did it! We got someone to listen, somebody who cared enough to get things changed!" Tommy burst out with a triumphant laugh. I imagined him on the other end of the phone, pacing around his kitchen, wearing an enormous grin. They both certainly sounded elated. Short and sweet, I delivered the good news to them and hung up. I had to move it and get on the road. There were so many people to call and so much celebrating to do!

I searched, fumbling through my purse for my car keys and walked out of the office.

"Ahh, there they are," I said to myself as I finally felt the soft pink and orange rubber flip-flop ornament hanging from the key chain, an ornament with Jennifer's name stamped on it.

I couldn't help thinking as I glanced toward the gift shop area of the lobby how God had just answered another prayer. Incredible! Prayer number seven was answered, practically wrapped up with a bow. At least, I thought it was number seven. It was difficult to keep count now and God just kept the blessings coming.

And then I saw her. She was standing with her back to me, gazing at the purses in the gift shop window. Her mid length dark brown hair hung down her back, and her slim, petite figure was slightly leaning in toward the glass. The blue jeans and black clunky heeled boots were unmistakable! My eyes darted toward the purses behind the glass, and I realized she was focused on the large sparkly, fake diamond crosses and pearls that adorned each one. Stopping in my tracks, I stared at her. Jennifer! I felt my heart float up toward my throat, and realized I was holding my breath. *How could it be…? How can she be here?*

I couldn't believe what I was seeing!

Swiveling around suddenly, she refocused her attention toward someone calling out to her, someone near me. I couldn't help noticing the silver wire-rimmed glasses she wore and felt the stabbing pain of a sweet image I'd filed away in my memory only a few years earlier. The glasses were so similar, even though Jenny didn't always wear hers. They looked much like Jennifer's, just as the girl herself looked a lot like Jennifer. She could have passed as Jennifer's twin in fact. But she wasn't *Jennifer*…

The realization felt like a gigantic cold snowball falling from the sky and landing on my entire body. It just flat wasn't Jennifer, and I was angry at myself for even entertaining the thought, even for a second, it could have been her. How did I fall for that again? I wanted it to be her, even deluded myself into thinking it *was* her for one small moment. And the extreme disappointment that it wasn't her was overwhelming. I felt my eyes fill up once again with tears.

"How many more times will this happen?" I admonished myself.

Walking as quickly as I could, I finally exited the hospital and let the tears fall freely when I sat behind the wheel of my car. A flashback of Jennifer visiting me at work several years before played through my mind. Just remembering how she'd sat near me at my desk waiting for Jake to pick her and Emma up made me feel better. Only moments before, she'd left her doctor's office and popped in for a quick visit, taking me completely by surprise.

"Hey, I'll walk you out to the parking garage since that's where he's picking you up," I'd offered. "He'll probably be here soon, won't he?"

"Yeah. I could use some help carrying this heavy stinker," she said as she struggled to pick up the baby carrier. "She's probably not helping my heart arrhythmia, huh?" she laughed.

"Uh, no. Not the way *she's* gaining weight and growing!" I agreed. "You know, babies should probably be carried on their mom's backs until they reach walking age, kinda like spiders. Those baby carriers are just too heavy to lug around! I'll carry her out there for you so you can have a rest."

Laughing at my comment, she accepted my offer and handed the carrier to me. Within a matter of only a few minutes, Jake pulled into the parking garage, and they left the hospital. My one and only visit from Jennifer at work…just a treasured memory now. But I couldn't forget the way she lit up when he arrived! She practically glowed with happiness as he parked the car and got out to help her load Emma's carrier into the backseat.

I wondered if he'd ever felt as crazy about her. I hoped so…but still…he was the man who wouldn't buy her a ring, wouldn't marry her, and wouldn't keep her heart from breaking. For whatever reason, he wouldn't, even though *she* believed he was the one for her, even though she'd attended couples counseling with him at their church and had two daughters with him.

The girl I'd seen at the hospital gift shop was still on my mind as I pulled into my driveway and shut off the car engine. How much she'd looked like Jenny! I reached toward the radio to turn it off and noticed the melody playing was a song I'd heard before but didn't really get to hear the words to. Listening closely, I was stunned by what I heard. It almost seemed I was meant to hear those exact words at that precise moment because they fit perfectly with my thoughts of Jenny and Jake.

Certain parts of the lyrics reminded me so much of the relationship between Jennifer and Jake that I wondered why I hadn't noticed those words before. They were about a young girl who is influenced by a young man she sees as her rescuer, a smooth talker who persuades her to succumb to his desires. As a result, it isn't a relationship that's healthy and good for her. The song just overall seemed to be about people searching for love and acceptance but going about it the wrong way. It reminded me that even though we knew Jenny was loved by her family, she'd also been searching for those things in an intimate relationship, as most people do.

I made a point to remember the song was performed by Casting Crowns, so I could research it on my computer. I already loved the name of the song "Does Anybody Hear Her?" and couldn't wait to buy it on CD.

What an incredible day I'd had! I closed my car door and slowly walked toward the porch of my house. The image of the girl I'd seen at the gift shop window flashed through my mind. Seeing her, hearing the song in my car, and having *Jenny's law* passed through legislation all in the same day was wonderfully overwhelming. It was apparent God was telling me something.

Lord, these have to be signs from you, and I thank you so much for them! I'm going to take those to mean you are pointing out your presence to me again and you're still comforting us. If you would, please let Jenny know the new law passed because I know she'd be thrilled something helpful to others came from her senseless death.

I had no idea if it was silly to ask God to give Jennifer a message, but I silently asked anyway. After all, he knows the desires of our hearts, and I knew it wouldn't hurt to ask.

I WONDER IF SHE KNOWS

"So, when does *Jenny's law* go into effect?" my sister Connie asked several evenings later. "I can't believe it passed. I'm so glad! You know Jennifer would be happy too."

I could hear her voice crack then a sniffle and eventually the sound of her blowing her nose into a tissue over the phone.

"July first," I replied. "And you're right. She'd be happy knowing she'd helped somebody. Poor girl! She really died in an awful way. But you know she's in heaven. I absolutely believe that. And she wouldn't want you or anybody else being miserable the rest of our lives," I told her. "I really believe that." Flipping back my bedroom window curtain, I noticed it was already dark outside.

"Yeah, I guess you're right," she agreed. "I know she didn't talk about her faith very often, but she *did* believe in God and Jesus, His Son. I know we'll see her again someday. I just wish we could see her *now*. There're so many things I wish I could tell her." Her voice trailed off wistfully.

The silence on the phone at that moment was deafening, and I imagined Connie rubbing her eyes, trying to compose herself. She was missing Jennifer horribly and having a bad day dealing with her own memories of Jenny and the relationship they'd shared.

"Hey, at least it's an easy date to remember," I feebly attempted to cheer her up. "July 1, 2008, it's a cool date! And it's the first day of the second half of the year. Anyone could remember that, right?" I joked. Still staring out the window, I noticed the stars looked particularly bright.

"Yeah, right. Like I'm gonna remember that date!" She laughed, blowing her nose once more. "I'm lucky I remember my own birthday these days."

"I know what you mean," I agreed. "Oh hey, I almost forgot to tell you. The governor's going to let our family attend a public 'mock' signing of *Jenny's law* at the capitol sometime this summer. Isn't that awesome? I talked to Tommy, and he's going to come back for it. We'll get to meet the governor and have our pictures taken with him too. So even though the law goes into effect on July first, we won't miss out on the 'official' signing of the bill. I'm so excited!"

"Man, that *is* neat! You know I probably won't get to go though. There's always something else going on… either with my kids or my grandkids," she said with an exasperated tone. "You guys go ahead and go and shake his hand for *me*." At the sound of her lighthearted laugh, I could tell she was feeling better already.

"I will, sis, but just remember this: Even though Jenny's gone, we can still be thankful for the twenty years we had with her. And we have to remember God returned her to us. Lots of families don't have that luxury. Some families never get their loved one's bodies back. God's been so good to us. He's been there every step of the way. And… oh wow! I just saw a falling star. Wouldn't it be great if it was a sign Jenny somehow knew we're talking about her?" I scanned the sky, looking for more heavenly objects heading toward our planet.

"Yes, it would be really cool!" she agreed, sounding elated at the thought. "Maybe it's her way of saying she misses us too."

How many more nights would we spend on the phone, missing Jennifer, together? When we ended our conversation, I thought of the amazing, different ways God answered our prayers. Through dreams, a forensic detective, a killer turning himself in, a discovered tape recording, the justice system, and a supportive, caring senator, our prayers were all answered. *My* prayers were answered. How could anyone say God isn't alive, isn't real, or doesn't care for us? I knew just the opposite was true. I just wish everyone knew it.

The morning of August 22, 2008, arrived at last! When I awoke, I felt the adrenaline rush through my body at the thought of the day's events ahead. Picking through my closet, I found the soft, cream-colored ruffled blouse I'd wear. Then I matched it up with a pair of black tuxedo-style dress pants. Perfect. Not too dressy and not too casual. I definitely wanted to be comfortable.

I felt myself break out in a sweat as I got dressed. I was excited and more nervous than I thought I'd be. Along with the anticipation of the day's events came one of those natural worries I'd trip as I walked toward the governor's desk. What if I stumbled, stuttered, or stood up at the wrong time?

"Don't think about it or it'll happen, Mary!" I told myself. No matter how hard I tried, I couldn't ease the butterflies in my stomach. After all, one didn't get to meet the governor every day. Plus I'd finally get to meet the senator who helped get the whole thing started. He'd be there, along with other legislative officials who would witness the signing of the new law. I thought about the other families who'd also be there, people who were *also* anxious to see the governor sign a law they were happy to have passed.

To most people in Oklahoma it's just another day, I thought. *But to our family and a few others, it's monumental. Thank you, Lord.*

I wished more family members could have attended the signing but understood their busy lives and routines were something they couldn't change. I'd been extremely busy myself, the week leading up to the signing. And Tommy arrived in Oklahoma only a day or two before the event, himself. As it worked out, the two of us were the only family who'd be attending the event.

I shut off the coffee pot before heading for the door and imagined my mom running errands later in the day for my sister Kim. She'd been helping her a lot lately. Whether picking up Kim's daughters at school or helping with other things, I knew keeping busy was a healthy outlet for Mom's sorrow after losing Jenny. Besides, Katie and Emma had recently started day care, and Mom had more free time. She knew Jennifer wouldn't want her moping all day, and Mom always helped when someone needed a hand. She sounded a little resigned lately, a little depressed and distant. I knew I just had to keep praying for her and talking to her about Jennifer. The one thing I'd learned since Jenny died is that people who lose someone to murder need to keep talking about their loved one. It helps keep the person alive. I discovered within myself, I didn't ever want to stop talking about her. It would almost make it seem like I'd forgotten her. And I couldn't, ever.

I practically skipped out the door into the merciless glare of the afternoon sun, more than ready to take the most significant ride to the capitol I knew I'd ever take.

Walking through the metal detector of the security checkpoint, I couldn't help noticing the other excited families, news media members, and legislators. Was I imagining it or did everyone in the entrance of the capitol seem more cheerful, like they were sharing in our family's happiness? High-pitched giggles and robust laughter echoed occasionally throughout the walkway just beyond the checkpoint. Surely there were families like ours meeting the governor for the first time. They had to be celebrating their *own* victories. As much as I'd have enjoyed sharing our moment with them all, I knew they each had their own agendas. After all, ours was just one of many bills that passed only a few months earlier.

"Where is the governor's blue room?" I heard one gentleman ask as he walked a few steps ahead of me.

"Up on the second floor, east side of the building," came the reply from a security guard. With the white flash of a wide smile, he pointed toward the hall, which led to the elevators. Good. I wouldn't have to ask for directions since it was my destination too.

"Hey, there you are!" Tommy called out to me as I rounded a corner and saw him pacing nervously near an elevator door. He caught it just in time, with a noticeable spring in his step, and held it open for me. The bright red "Oklahoma Has Jenny's Law" button stood out boldly against the gray of his button-up dress shirt. How thrilled he looked...and yet so composed!

I knew he was churning inside though, just as I was. We'd both rather be somewhere else, doing something different *with Jennifer still in our lives*. But it wasn't to be. The door to that alternate possible future was forever closed, slammed shut by Ron. He'd made sure he sealed it shut.

"Are you ready for this?" Tommy asked as we exited the elevator and stood outside the "blue room." Crowds of people hurriedly rushed past us and found their way to seats just inside the door. I couldn't help noticing Tommy's eyes, so much like Jennifer's. They glistened with tears, but this time they were tears of *joy*! Something positive was actually coming out of Jenny's death and we couldn't have been more thankful.

"Yes, I'm ready for this!" I exclaimed, a bit loudly. "I feel like we've waited years for this day even though it actually happened pretty fast. Just think of everything we've been through since Jenny disappeared. In a way, it seems like we've waited a lifetime for *Jenny's law*."

"Yeah, it does to me too," Tommy agreed distractedly, his eyes darting toward the elevator door. "Hey, I think Senator Reynolds is coming this way. Remember we saw him at the tree-lighting ceremony we went to after we buried Jenny? I'm pretty sure that's him."

"Where?" I asked, searching the crowd as it moved in our direction. "Oh, I see him!"

The senator approached the doorway, extending his arm toward Tommy and gave him a firm handshake and pat on the back. Standing a few inches taller than Tommy, he towered over my short frame.

"Tommy?" he asked.

"That's me!" Tommy laughed, returning the handshake. "Man, I'm glad you could make it!"

"And Mary, right?" He smiled warmly, his sky blue eyes lighting up his face.

"Yes, I'm the one who's been pestering your assistant these past several months," I said with a nervous laugh. "I confess I'm guilty. I only hope I didn't drive your assistant nuts!" The blush spread across my face, and I hoped I didn't look as nervous as I felt.

"No…I'm sure you didn't." He smiled as if to say, "Relax." "She's used to people contacting our office. She understands people get excited, especially about things they're passionate about."

His genuine warmth and concern for our family was obvious. It practically flowed out of the guy! And because of his openness, I imagined him talking with his own family about our Jennifer, the story of her disappearance, and her eventual burial. I also imagined him wondering just how horrible it would be to have lost a daughter in the same manner. He truly seemed to care and realize we'd been through an unbelievable grief, one so many families experience in this day and time.

"I'm so sorry for your loss of Jennifer…," the senator said softly, glancing from Tommy to me. "I wish there wasn't a need for a law like this, and I wish there were something else I could do to make things better." His entire being radiated sincerity.

"Hey, we just appreciate what you've done. It's not every day someone can get a law passed. We're really grateful you took the time to listen to our story. And so many other families will be able to benefit from this law.

Unfortunately, ours won't be the last one to have to deal with something like this," Tommy pointed out.

"That's so true." I jumped into the conversation with an emphatic nod. "Oh hey. Not to change the topic, but it looks like it's almost time for the governor to come in, and this room is really filling up. Maybe we should go grab a seat before they're all gone," I suggested, looking inside the room at the rows of people already seated.

"Yep, you're right about that," Tommy agreed. "We'd better roll in before we get left out..." His voice trailed off as he took in the view upon entering the room.

The view inside the room was breathtaking! The walls, the floors, every inch of the "blue room" shouted "elegant business" décor. A calming shade of cornflower blue covered the wall, its perfect seam flowing directly into the beautifully ornate white of the window frames. Lush gold dressings framed the windows, allowing the optimal amount of sunlight to flood the room and illuminate it. Gazing upward, I noticed the white raised ceiling sporting an exquisite chandelier in the center of the room, just another touch of elegance giving a softer touch to the room. The same cornflower blue was strategically placed throughout the room, clearly evident in the furniture, rugs, and other pieces of décor.

The "showstopper," however, had to be the gorgeous white marble-looking fireplace located at the front of the room. *Wow! I wouldn't mind having it in my house!* The huge mirror positioned directly above it reflected the image of the twinkling chandelier and the wall near the room's entrance. It was an overwhelmingly beautiful room, and I knew I would remember this forever.

"Hey girl! There you are!" I heard as I pulled my gaze away from the fireplace and looked back toward the doorway. My friends Shelba and Holly worked their way toward me, immediately giving me a hug.

"Oh wow! Am I glad you guys made it!" I flashed a smile at them.

"We wouldn't miss this day with you for anything, Mary," Shelba reassured me.

"Yeah, and we remembered our cameras!" Holly added, holding up the shiny silver camera for my inspection.

"Well, we really appreciate you guys being here. It's a major honor for our family and a great achievement for homicide families!" I hoped I wouldn't break down and cry as I thanked them for showing up.

"Yes, it is. And the families down the road will be so grateful for this law if their loved one's body is mistreated like Jennifer's was," Shelba pointed out. The warmth and depth of her caring was immensely comforting, and I considered myself extremely blessed they were both my friends.

Introductions were made within our small group, and we soon found our seats, chattering softly among ourselves. *If only Jennifer could see this day, this room, this group of anxious people! But then if she could witness this, she'd still be alive. She'd be here, and there'd be no "Jenny's law."* How I wished that was the case!

Still...what if? What if God somehow let Jennifer know? I didn't know for a fact he *wouldn't*. So much of life beyond the grave was a mystery!

"Ladies and gentlemen, please stand as we present the honorable governor of the state of Oklahoma..."

Nearly popping up from my seat, I joined other anxious Oklahomans who stood and stared toward the entrance near the fireplace.

He was here!

He entered the room smiling and looking very relaxed. His face beamed as he began shaking the hands of a few crowd members. Yes, this was the governor I'd seen on TV on many news telecasts. He appeared just as pleasant and personable as I'd imagined him.

God bless this man who saw and agreed with the need for Jenny's law! And most of all, thank you, Lord, for his role in helping us get this law passed. It is just one more answered prayer. Amen!

"I wish Jenny knew what was going on here today," Tommy whispered as he leaned toward me, looking happy one moment then sad the next.

The memory of the star that fell through the sky while I talked with my sister Connie on the phone, not long ago, suddenly came to me. We were curious, saying it could be her sending us a message, a message she was still aware and still loved us. I'll always wonder about the star.

"I have a feeling somehow she knows," I whispered back to Tommy with more peace in my heart and faith in my soul than I'd ever possessed before. "I really *do*…" My voice trailed off as I refocused on the announcements being made. In fact, our names were being called to come forward for photo opportunities with the governor and to witness him signing *Jenny's law,* an enactment witnessed by more than ourselves.

Hebrews 12:1. (NIV): Therefore, since we are surrounded by such a great cloud of witnesses…

Matthew 19:26. (NIV): Jesus looked at them and said, "With man this is impossible, but with God all things are possible."

JENNY'S LAW

SENATE BILL 1992 ~ SECTION 6 "JENNY'S LAW"

Section 6 of this act shall be known and may be cited as "Jenny's Law".

SECTION 6. NEW LAW A new section of law to be codified in the Oklahoma Statutes as Section 1161.1 of Title 21, unless there is created a duplication in numbering, reads as follows:

A. It is unlawful for any person to knowingly and willfully desecrate a human corpse for any purpose of:

1. Tampering with the evidence of a crime;
2. Camouflaging the death of human being;
3. Disposing of a dead body;
4. Impeding or prohibiting the detection, investigation or prosecution of a crime;
5. Altering, inhibiting or concealing the identification of a dead body, a crime victim, or a criminal offender; or
6. Disrupting, prohibiting or interfering with any law enforcement agency or the Office of the State

Medical Examiner in detecting, investigating, examining, determining, identifying or processing a dead body, cause of death, the scene where a dead body is found, or any forensic examination or investigation relating to a dead body or a crime.

B. Upon conviction, the violator of any provision of this section shall be guilty of a felony punishable by imprisonment in the custody of the Department of Corrections for a term not more than seven (7) years, by a fine not exceeding Eight Thousand Dollars ($8,000.00), or by both such fine and imprisonment.

C. This offense may be prosecuted in addition to any prosecution pursuant to Section 1161 of Title 21 of the Oklahoma Statutes for removal of a dead body or any other criminal offense.

D. For purposes of this section, "desecration of a human corpse" means any act committed after the death of a human being including, but not limited to, dismemberment, disfigurement, mutilation, burning, or any act committed to cause the dead body to be devoured, scattered or dissipated; except, those procedures performed by a state agency or licensed authority in due course of its duties and responsibilities for forensic examination, gathering or removing crime scene evidence, presentation or preservation of evidence, dead body identification, cause of death, autopsy, cremation or burial, organ donation, use of a cadaver for medical educational purposes, or other necessary procedures to identify, remove or dispose of a dead body by the proper authority.

SECTION 7. This act shall become effective July 1, 2008.

Mock signing of 'Jenny's Law.' Left to right: State Rep. Anastasia Pittman, Senator Jim Reynolds, author M.K. Howard, Governor Brad Henry, & Tommy Sipes

ACKNOWLEDGMENTS

During the heartbreaking sorrow our family experienced after and throughout our loss of Jennifer, many people supported and shared in our pain. In fact, they helped ease our burden by simply standing with us during remembrance events, phoning to check in on us and even sharing in graveside birthday remembrances for Jennifer. One of those people is Jim Reynolds, the Senator who drafted and was successful in getting "Jenny's Law" passed. His compassionate concern and drive to get the law passed will always be remembered by our family.

The Oklahoma County District Attorney's office also holds a special place within our family's hearts. David Prater, Gary Ackley, Scott Rowland, and Shelba Norris have been particularly helpful in guiding us through the justice system and in supporting crime victims. Their steadfast assistance to our community is invaluable. Thank you so much to the entire staff for your tireless work.

Most recently, I'd like to give a huge hug and sincere "thank you" to my dear friend, Aliph Peterson, for her encouragement and assistance during the writing of this book. Both her patience and eagerness to see it through to the end are truly appreciated.

I pray God blesses each of you and thank you all for being the wonderful and inspiring people you are!

M.K. Howard

CREDITS

I would like to thank the following artists and/or corporations for graciously allowing me to reference their works within this book. All rights are reserved by the copyright owners to the following items:

Burgeis, Robert. "PromiseLand (Jenny's Song)". Robert Burgeis, 2006. CD. (song)

Bickley, William & Warren, Michael (Writers). Family Matters. Television. Executive Producers: Thomas L. Miller & Robert L. Boyett. 1989. ABC.